It Scrapped

Get It Scrapped!

Organize, Visualize, Create

Debbie Hodge

Memory Makers Books
Cincinnati, Ohio
www.mycraftivity.com

12 11 10 09 08   5 4 3 2 1

Distributed in Canada by Fraser Direct

100 Armstrong Avenue

Georgetown, ON, Canada L7G 5S4

Tel: (905) 877-4411

Distributed in the U.K. and Europe by David & Charles

Brunel House, Newton Abbot, Devon, TQ12 4PU, England

Tel: (+44) 1626 323200, Fax: (+44) 1626 323319

E-mail: postmaster@davidandcharles.co.uk

Distributed in Australia by Capricorn Link

P.O. Box 704, S. Windsor, NSW 2756 Australia

Tel: (02) 4577-3555

Library of Congress Cataloging-in-Publication Data
Hodge, Debbie

  Get it scrapped! / Debbie Hodge.

    p. cm.

  Includes index.

  ISBN 978-1-59963-015-1 (softcover : alk. paper)

1. Photograph albums. 2. Scrapbooks. I. Title.

TR501.H63 2008

745.593--dc22

                    2007043941

Metric Conversion Chart

to convert	to	multiply by
Inches	Centimeters	2.54
Centimeters	Inches	0.4
Feet	Centimeters	30.5
Centimeters	Feet	0.03
Yards	Meters	0.9
Meters	Yards	1.1
Sq. Inches	Sq. Centimeters	6.45
Sq. Centimeters	Sq. Inches	0.16
Sq. Feet	Sq. Meters	0.09
Sq. Meters	Sq. Feet	10.8
Sq. Yards	Sq. Meters	0.8
Sq. Meters	Sq. Yards	1.2
Pounds	Kilograms	0.45
Kilograms	Pounds	2.2
Ounces	Grams	28.3
Grams	Ounces	0.035

F+W PUBLICATIONS, INC.

Editor: Amy Glander

Interior Designer: Corrie Schaffeld

Cover Designer: Jeremy Werling

Art Coordinator: Eileen Aber

Production Coordinator: Matt Wagner

Photographer: Tim Grondin

Stylist: Jan Nickum

www.fwpublications.com

DEDICATION

This book is dedicated to Neil, Joshua and Isaac, who not only believe in me and celebrate my work, but who come up with great scrapbook page and title ideas.

ACKNOWLEDGMENTS

I am very grateful to these companies for their sponsorship of this book: American Crafts, American Traditional Designs, Crate Paper, Fancy Pants Designs, Heidi Grace Designs/Fiskars, Mustard Moon, Prima, Prism, Sakura and Urban Lily.

A huge thanks goes out to the book's contributors, Kim Kesti, Betsy Veldman and Sharyn Tormanen for the thought and craftsmanship they put into their pages. Sharyn, especially, took the themes of this book to heart, and I'm immensely grateful for her advice and smart, good humor.

Many thanks to Christine Doyle, who saw this book's potential, Amy Glander who helped shape it, Corrie Schaffeld for "the look," and Eileen Aber for numerous acts of support, big and small.

Finally, thank you to Hillary Heidelberg for her cyber-companionship and generous, smart friendship as I wrote this book. Special appreciation to my online scrapping friends: Sara Dickey, Séverine di Giacomo, Paula Gilarde, Roxanne Jegotdka, Deanna Kroll, Lori Mar, Jennifer Mayer, Betsy Sammarco, Doris Sander and Celeste Smith.

Table of Contents

So many photos...so little time

Digital cameras, cell phone cameras, online sharing, and easy scanning of older and vintage photos are all resulting in what can be a staggering number of photos to make sense of and preserve.

If you're overwhelmed, feeling guilty or perhaps just plain motivated to winnow them down and get the shots you love into albums, read on and find out how you can *get it scrapped!*

When you've got a basic organizational routine, everything seems easier—because it is. Chapter One gives suggestions on how you can be ready to scrap as the urge or opportunity arises by having an ongoing plan for staging your photos.

The remainder of the book is structured around "page types." There are several typical page types that most of us scrap, each with its own requirements and opportunities. Once you understand these—Events, Moments, Yourself, Everyday Life, Collections and Your World—you can get to the heart of your pages while getting them scrapped.

Debbie Hodge

Chapter 1
Get Organized

Each of us has our own work style.

Take the example of laundry. I'm a batcher when it comes to laundry. I don't do it on any given schedule. While I admire my sister-in-law, who keeps on top of things, washing and hanging out a load or two every day, my approach is different. I have four hampers (whites, darks, colors and specials). I do laundry when any of the following happen: A hamper is full, one of us is out of something or I feel like it. And at that point I'll probably do several loads, washing and folding all day as I do other things. Sure we run out of things occasionally, but all the laundry does get done every week or so.

Either of these approaches can be taken with scrapbooking. As long as you have a basic organization (like my laundry hampers), you don't have to be caught up and putting photos into albums chronologically to ensure that you "get it scrapped!"

Basic Page Formats

You can scrap photos—at a minimum—with paper, photos, adhesive, scissors and a pen. A first decision to make is what size paper you'll use as your page canvas. Your most common choices include:

8" x 8" or smaller (20cm x 20cm or smaller)	Good for gift albums or focused theme or event albums.
8½" x 11" or 12" x 12" (22cm x 28cm or 30cm x 30cm)	Making personal and family albums is easiest with these formats. They present enough space for photos, title and journaling. They store well in the average home, and products are widely available. You can also store both sizes in many of the 12" x 12" (30cm x 30cm) albums on the market.
18" x 18" or larger (46cm x 46cm or larger)	Oversized albums make a great statement. Be prepared to spend more money on your supplies and a bit more time tracking them down. Make sure you can store albums this size in a cool, dry spot.
Pocket page (Varying sizes)	Purchase pocket pages the same size as your chosen album format and integrate scrapped pages with photos presented this way.

If you're just getting started in scrapbooking or are just wanting to consider your options, the place to start is with the basic album. Begin by considering size and binding when selecting an album that fits your taste and style.

- Use albums that accommodate top-load page protectors into which you can slide your finished, scrapped pages. Use an album size that will work with your chosen page size(s). Look for the ability to easily reorder your pages.

- D-ring albums hold both 12" x 12" (30cm x 30cm) and 8½" x 11" (22cm x 28cm) page protectors. To accommodate 8½" x 11" (22cm x 28cm) landscape pages, trim a 12" x 12" (30cm x 30cm) protector to 12" x 8½" (30cm x 22cm). D-ring albums are the easiest to open and reorder pages, but a little clunky to handle, and when you make two-page layouts, the middle seams don't abut closely.

- EZ-Load, postbound and strap-hinge systems all keep the pages more securely bound and join two-page layouts nicely. The trade-off is in the ease of loading and changing the order of pages.

This 12" x 12" (30cm x 30cm) D-ring binder holds my scrapped pages of various sizes as well as photo-pocket pages and memorabilia pockets. With this kind of flexibility available, I decided to scrap the biggest moment of the Lee Fair for us—when Isaac won a first-place trophy in the pedal tractor pull—and then put the many supporting photos that he loves looking at in a facing pocket page.

There are a variety of page "types" that you will scrap — from playful multi-photo event spreads to endearing one-shot moment pages.

Get It Scrapped! is organized around six basic page types that are described on the next page with suggestions specific to each. Before you dig into these individual types, though, here's an overall approach for getting all of your photos staged and ready. In this chapter I'll describe the things you need to do in an ongoing way so that periodically you can stage photos to be scrapped as you like.

What?

Shoot, cull and store.

Identify, flag and stage.

Scrap!

When?

Ongoing

Periodically

As you like

My kids adore Halloween, and this two-page layout showcases their love for this annual holiday. See Chapter 2 for more event layouts.

We all have trinkets and treasures that mean the world to us. See chapter 7 for more examples of ways to document the things or places that are a part of your world.

How you get your pages scrapped is influenced by their content.

Understand these basic page types and use the information in chapters 2–7 to speed up your process for each page type.

Events: Birthday parties, vacations, school ceremonies, holidays, park outings, family hikes and travel all fall into this category.

Moments: These are the pages showcasing photos, insights and messages that compel you.

Yourself: The facts about yourself as well as your feelings, habits, achievements and outlook on life can be ever-changing and a joy to reflect on.

Everyday Life: Around the house, hanging out with friends, recording the garden's progress, little stories and routines are the heart of any album.

Collections: Photos that don't stand on their own but that work in over-time, themed or lineup-type collections give you pages that reveal trends.

Your World: What did your childhood home look like? What about the town you grew up in, or the dishes your family ate off for years? Take everyday life one step further by leaving a record of the life you lived in the past as well as the life you are living now.

This page shares a heartwarming narrative about why home is so important. See chapter 7 for inspiration on ways to document the world around you.

The first step in getting your photos scrapped is to organize them. There are three things you need to do in an ongoing way:

1) Shoot
Keep your camera batteries charged, take photos and get them processed.

2) Cull
Sort through your photos (both print and digital) and toss out those that you do not need or want. Not only will this save you space, it will save you time, and in the end you will have albums with a more specific focus. Get rid of photos that are of poor quality, that are not relevant to your topic or theme or are close to duplicates of the ones you want to keep.

3) Store
Use a storage system (like my laundry hampers) that will protect your photos and provide a basic organization that makes it quick and easy to find photos and get them scrapped.

Tips for Storing Prints

- Use acid-free boxes.

- Label outside of box with date range stored: YYYY MM to YYYY MM.

- Use a tabbed index card for every shoot/event labeled YYYY MM SUBJECT. (See page 21 for more tips on storage once you are ready to get them scrapped.)

If you are shooting digitally, you have two organizational tasks. The first is to organize your files; the second is to organize your prints. Here are some tips for organizing and storing your digital files.

Folders

☐ 📂 Photos
  ⊞ 📁 2002
  ⊞ 📁 2003
  ⊞ 📁 2004
  ⊞ 📁 2005
  ⊞ 📁 2006
  ☐ 📁 2007
    ⊞ 📁 2007 01
    ⊞ 📁 2007 02
    ⊞ 📁 2007 03
    ⊞ 📁 2007 04
    ☐ 📁 2007 05
      ⊞ 📁 2007 05 AtHome
      ⊞ 📁 2007 05 Cinco de Mayo Party
      ⊞ 📁 2007 05 Debbie Birthday
      ⊞ 📁 2007 05 Isaac Chorus Concert
      ⊞ 📁 2007 05 Joshua Band Concert
      ⊞ 📁 2007 05 Memorial Day
      ⊞ 📁 2007 05 School May Fair

• Do not rename files. Instead, name the folders they are in for easy and meaningful retrieval. Organizational software can also provide easy indexing identification.

• Store photos for each shoot/event in their own folder using a folder-naming strategy that results in a chronological sort on your computer. A great way to do this is with a four-digit year space, two-digit month space subject. This tree shows a method in which there is one folder for each year. Within the year folders there are folders for each month. And within each month, there are folders for each shoot/event/subject. I keep the naming structure all the way down the tree for easy identification at any point.

Make it Easy

Integrate the prints and digital photos you receive from other sources—friends' online sharing, scanned photos, etc.—into your system, using chronologically labeled folders and tabbed index cards to mix them in.

Organize photos and plan pages.

How frequently you do this will vary depending on the volume of photos you take and the rhythms of your life. I take many photos every month, but there are often seasonal overlaps that I like to consider. I usually take care of September, October and November just before Thanksgiving as one group because there are all kinds of school photos and fall activities that overlap. The summer months are another chunk I like to process as a group. So pull out your groups of photos and browse in order to:

1) Identify

Identify groups of photos to scrap together. These will often be Event and Everyday Life photos. Get an idea of whether you'll put these photos on one- or two-page layouts, on multiple layouts, or maybe in pocket pages. List each planned page.

Example:

I "batched" my recent May and June photos together because I knew there was overlap in end-of-school activities, baseball shoots and around-the-house shots I took.

Because I use digital photos, I browsed through them with photo-organization software to get an idea of what I have. With prints, I would thumb through them.

This shows eight May folders and six June folders.

I came up with a plan to get these photos into albums that calls for more than ten scrapped pages and several groupings put into pocket pages.

From the May and June "At Home" folders

- An everyday life layout of neighborhood play (with photos from May and June).
- A moment page of Isaac learning guitar.
- A moment page of Joshua getting glasses.
- An everyday life layout of "breaking out the slip-n-slide."
- Two or three pocket pages with around-the-house photos.

From the May and June "Baseball" folders

- A two-page event layout combining May and June photos.
- A collection layout combining a portrait of my son with photos from baseball and soccer games earlier in the year.

From the Cinco de Mayo folder

- The photos ended up being mostly portraits of my husband and myself, and I flagged them for future moment and yourself pages.

From my May birthday folder

- A one-page event layout.

From the Memorial Day folder

- A two-page event layout.
- Pocket pages to follow the layout in the album for the photos I took of the many families.

From multiple end-of-school folders

- A two-page "End of Fifth Grade" Collections layout for Joshua, combining his concert photos and party photos, as well as some from an April field trip.
- A two-page "End of Second Grade" Collections layout for Isaac, combining his concert, May Fair and field trip photos.

From Isaac's birthday folder

- A two-page event layout from the birthday party.
- A one-page layout from our home celebration—gifts and cake.

From Molasses Pond party folder

- A two-page layout from this annual retreat with my writing friends.

Make it Easy

Once you get an initial plan for pages to scrap, check them out for "doability." If something seems like too big of a job, try one of these scrapping alternatives.

- Put a whole event in pocket pages; slide journaling and title into their own pockets.

- Upload photos from a large event or related shoots and have a bound book made.

2) Flag

Flag photos to scrap with those from other shoots on collection pages. These are often photos that you'd rather not give an entire page, but that you do want to get into your album. If you know what you're doing with this right now, list the page. If you're in the early stages of collecting, flag and/or file the photo(s). Examples of collections I'm building are: "kids with Grandpa," "neighborhood play," "best friends" and "Joshua's creations."

• If you're working with prints, flag by pulling and filing in the appropriate box.

• If you're working with digital photos, use photo-organization software to leave photos where they are on your hard drive but reference them in digital categories or albums.

Joshua, 2004 is when you are eight years old & in 3rd grade. You're kind to many-especially your little brother. Your grown-up teeth are coming in but your mouth hasn't caught up. Toward the end of this year, you started changing from a being a skinny guy to a hustler one.

Using Google's free photo-organization software, Picasa, I "flagged" throughout 2004 several photos of my son that I really liked and put them in a virtual album that helped me track them down for printing and scrapping on a collection page of him for 2004.

3) Stage

Staging entails getting the photos printed, grouped and easily accessible for scrapping. The approach you use will vary depending on whether you work with a film or digital camera.

Film camera and prints

For every layout you identified in your browsing, pull the photos. File each layout's photos together behind a tabbed index card in a box of "photos to be scrapped." File the photos that you flagged for future collection, moment or other pages behind appropriately labeled index cards. Keep this in your box of "photos being collected/held."

Digital camera and files

For every layout you identified in your browsing, crop and edit the needed photos in image-editing software. Order or print photos, and then file them in boxes as described above.

My biological clock never ticked. I never longed to have children, and when Neil and I got married, we still weren't really sure about us and parenthood and the responsibilities that looked overwhelming. And then . . . we had the wonderful experience of . . . YOU TWO! You two, who give me delight and love and pride and, yes, overwhelming responsibility. . . YOU TWO who connect me to life and this family in the most satisfying way possible. I love being your mom. 2006.

Supplies: Cardstock (Bazzill); chipboard scroll, patterned paper (Fancy Pants); rub-ons (BasicGrey); chipboard letter (Heidi Swapp); flowers (Heidi Swapp, Queen & Co.); Misc: Another Typewriter font

This photo taken at a local corn maze could have fit into one of several categories. When I was in the staging process, I decided to group it with moment photos because it evokes so much emotion and personal meaning to me.

Storing Staged Photos

Keep and label a separate acid-free storage box (or series of boxes) for the following (consider using different colors for each):

1) Photos as they come from the printer, unbrowsed and unstaged, filed in chronological order with tabbed index cards for each shoot.

2) "Photos to be scrapped." Use an envelope or tabbed index card to identify each planned layout's date and subject.

3) "Photos being collected/held." Use tabbed index cards to identify categories: i.e., "portraits of Isaac," "brother shots posed," "brother shots candid."

The following six chapters in *Get It Scrapped!* provide tips, advice and examples for getting each of six page types into your albums and include organizational and creative tips specific to each. Begin by selecting your page type and then turn to the appropriate chapter. Each chapter advises on:

Understanding just what you want on your page;

Picturing the page and selecting the right photos for it;

Telling the story of the page; and

Arranging the elements of each page, including title, journaling, photos and sometimes even memorabilia.

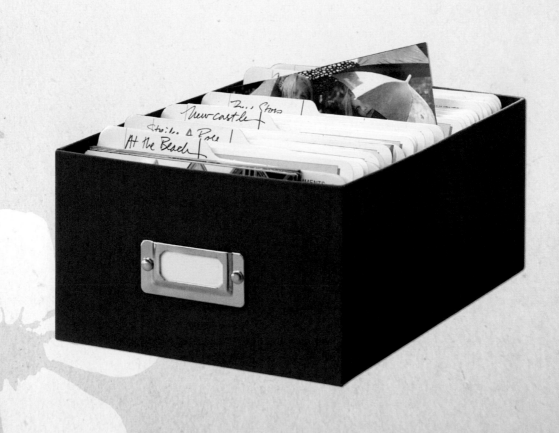

Supplies: Cardstock (Bazzill, Prism); epoxy circles, metal hat, patterned paper (American Traditional); chipboard circles (Bazzill); photo turn (7gypsies); brads (Making Memories); tag (Scrapworks); Misc: Century Gothic, Herald Square, Marcelle Script and Marcelle Swashes fonts, ink, transparency

Featured above is one of my all-time favorite event layouts. Before I started the page, I considered each of the four elements of scrapping to be sure I was capturing the entire event in the best way possible.

Understanding: I wanted a layout that showed the whole party, but that put my son in the spotlight.

Picturing: I selected two focal photos of my sons to print large and then grouped many smaller supporting photos.

Telling: I didn't have a lot of room, so I focused on the details that weren't in the photos and that I thought we'd most enjoy remembering in years to come—the party theme and Isaac's development of it as well as the brief thunder and lightning storm.

Arranging: The title, journaling and photos of the birthday boy, his brother and father all sit on the orange, landscape-oriented canvas that immediately draws the viewer's eye. The supporting photos are left unmatted and aligned in a vertical block that keeps the layout easy to navigate.

Chapter 2

Get *Events* Scrapped

A substantial portion of your photos are probably from events:

birthday parties, school ceremonies, church and community events, holidays, day trips, family outings, annual get-togethers and reunions, vacations and more. We all like to record these happenings—and usually by taking more than one or two photos. If you're the family shutterbug you probably have a wealth of event photos to choose from. So where to begin? Fear not. This chapter offers an easy process that will help you know what you have and get a page-by-page plan for getting all of your important events scrapped.

Organizing Event Photos

Step 1

Scope it out

Events come in different sizes—from the five shots of Grandpa having cake with the grandkids to the several hundred that may cover a typical Christmas season. The first step is to figure out how many photos you have from an event and just what they are.

Step 2

Break it down

The scope will determine how you break it down for a plan. Look for a logical grouping of photos if you are doing more than one page from the event. Think also of how the layouts will be sequenced within your album.

If you have:	You can:
1 or 2 photos	Make a one-page layout that marks the event's occurrence and conveys its essence. **-or-** Group these photos with others that have something in common with them (maybe other onesies from this season or photos from the same event in other years) and make a collection layout. See Chapter 4 for collection layout ideas.
several photos	Make a one- or two-page multi-photo layout.
many photos, covering multiple days	Make a series of layouts. Plan for logical groupings and sequencing. Plus: Another option is to scrap some of the photos and put the rest of the photos in pocket pages that fit in your album.

scope it out

After Halloween 2006, I had four folders of digital photos: Ervin Costume Party, Trick-or-Treat, School Parties and Pumpkins. I looked through them using photo-organization software and came up with this plan: 1) The photos from the adult costume party will go on a two-page layout. 2) The pumpkin photos will go on two one-page layouts—one of each of my sons and their pumpkin carvings. 3) The school party photos will go onto a single two-page spread. 4) The trick-or-treat photos will go on a one-page layout of my boys dressed up and a two-page layout of them trick-or-treating. (See "Halloween Face" on page 38.)

a part of the whole

This one-page layout of my youngest son carving his pumpkin will go in our family album facing a page of my older son doing the same activity. They'll be followed by spreads of trick-or-treating and parties. When you "scope it out" and "break it down," the result is a doable list of pages that tell the stories of your events.

Supplies: Cardstock (Bazzill); chipboard letters and shapes, felt shapes, letter stickers, patterned paper (American Crafts)

Since the scope of events can vary so widely, take a few minutes before making each layout to ask yourself:

* What story do I want to tell on this layout? Is it the story of the entire event, or of one activity or moment from the event, or is it somewhere between the two?

* Who is this layout really for? Is it my own record of what went on? Is it to show friends what my experience was? Is it for family now? Family later?

Let the answers to these questions guide your photo selections and journaling.

cooking with friends on Thanksgiving

I wasn't really on top off things when everyone arrived for Thanksgiving dinner, and I screwed up some of the stuff, and I don't think any of the kids ate more than one bite of turkey---yet I had a wonderful time. I think that it has to do with who my friends are and how our accumulated years of friendship have made each of us more accepting of and kind to each other. I'm guessing I was relaxed because I knew that they'd all bring lots of food and that Jill would cut up my squash and Elaine would keep an eye on everything in the oven in case I got distracted. Robin, who'd been sad about her older daughters not being in town, later said, "And I ended up feeling like I was with family." Here I'm making MY favorite gravy and Elaine is making HER favorite gravy and Lucy is stirring and Jill is in the back taking care of the squash.

November 2006

Me, Jill, Lucy, Elaine (making gravies)

Photos: Neil Niman

a holiday moment

In addition to a two-page spread that shows the whole event, pick out a favorite moment from a holiday celebration and scrap it. Write journaling that conveys the spirit of the moment by including selected details (just a few will trigger the rest) and bits of conversation. This layout is really for me, while the kids will appreciate the two-pager with lots of photos.

Supplies: Cardstock (Prism); patterned paper (American Crafts); clip (Heidi Swapp); ribbons (Heidi Grace); button (Autumn Leaves); chipboard (Pressed Petals); rub-on (Fancy Pants); Misc: Century Gothic and Desyrel fonts

The photos you have from events often direct what kind of story you tell in your layout. In deciding which photos to include, understand that your job is not to put as many photos as possible onto the page, but rather to put the right photos on it. Consider using some of your best shots—perhaps a familiar landmark or a stunning portrait of a family member—as the focus of your page.

Keep photos that show

* people key to your event

* relevant items
  (such as a birthday cake)

* key activities

* a sense of place

Wean out

* close duplicates

* photos of poor quality

* photos that don't
  contribute to your story

reduction plan

While we took many photos at Water Country, these five—along with the journaling—capture the essence of the entire outing. The people (us!), the equipment, our mood and even the weather are immediately understood through this column of 4" x 6" (10cm x 15cm) photos that have been trimmed to varying heights. Reduce your own outings to a limited number of photos that tell the whole story and you'll get your event pages scrapped more efficiently.

Supplies: Cardstock (Bazzill, Prism); patterned paper (A2Z, Autumn Leaves); die-cut letters (Provo Craft); rhinestones (Darice); date brush by Katie Pertiet (Designer Digitals); report card brush by Sande Krieger (Two Peas in a Bucket); Misc: Courier New and Felix Titling font, ink

Journaling events requires a combination of facts, details, stories and personal impressions. The journaling will come easier with some aids:

* Photograph small details even if you don't think the photo will make it into the album.

* Keep a journal (on paper, on your hard drive or even in a blog) of impressions and stories.

* Maintain memorabilia binders. Every January, fill a three-ring binder with an index tab for each month of the upcoming year and several empty page protectors. As the events happen, tuck invitations, tickets, brochures and other memorabilia into individual pockets and label each pocket accordingly. When you're ready to scrap the event, just pull the pocket for a supply of facts and memorabilia for the page.

repeating history

Sometimes the dry details are important. I vaguely knew that Fort William Henry was used in the novel *The Last of the Mohicans*. When I visited the fort myself, I wasn't sure if the soldiers who had manned this fort were British or French, and I couldn't remember how their demise came about. Save brochures from your vacation destinations (or look up the details on-line later). When your event is something with historical detail, get that into your journaling alongside the personal story.

Supplies: Patterned paper (7gypsies, Imaginisce, Scenic Route); metal letters (Jo-Ann); rub-on letters (Creative Imaginations); letter stickers (Li'l Davis); epoxy square (Autumn Leaves); transparency (My Mind's Eye); photo turn (7gypsies); photo corner (EK Success); Misc: Roman Serif font, brad, key charm, twine

Events often mean lots of photos. When you've got a multitude of photos you want to include on a page or spread, here are a few tips to remember as you're getting everything in order.

* Keep in mind you'll need ample space for the focal photo, supporting photos, title and journaling.

* Pick a photo to emphasize. Look for a way to set it apart from the others such as by size, matting, and/or its position on the page.

* Look for ways to group supporting photos logically. Possibilities include by activity (such as building a sandcastle, wave surfing or sun bathing), or by time (such as Easter preparations, an egg hunt or dinner).

* Use matting, cropping, and alignment to unite related groups of photos on the page

a place for everything

The enlarged focal photo in "The Hannukah Brawl" below makes it clear what holiday is being celebrated even without the title. Supporting photos are cropped to a uniform height and arranged to reveal the chronology of an "incident" during the celebration. The journaling block tells the details for those album-gazers who want to know more.

Supplies: Cardstock (Bazzill, Prism); patterned paper (Frances Meyer); die-cut letters and symbol (Provo Craft); rub-ons (Hambly); Misc: ITC Franklin Gothic font, ink

Large parties, small get-togethers and milestone ceremonies all belong in your albums.
Use titles that inform, colors that enhance the celebration theme and mood, and photos arranged to tell the story.

stay focused

Create a focal-point block even when all of your photos are the same 4" x 6" (10cm x 15cm) size. Here, two key photos—one of the birthday cake and another of the guests of honor blowing out candles—are set apart by the following touches. These photos are: 1) matted in white cardstock; 2) aligned into a portrait block; 3) backed by patterned paper; and 4) positioned near center. These small touches set them apart from the others and give the story immediate focus.

Supplies: Cardstock (Prism); patterned paper (KI Memories, Urban Lily); chipboard words, label plate, tag (Li'l Davis); chipboard numbers (We R Memory Keepers); chipboard accents (Creative Imaginations, Magistical Memories); rub-ons (Autumn Leaves, My Mind's Eye); strip stickers (Provo Craft); ribbon (May Arts); ribbon slide (Maya Road); decorative tape, photo turn (7gypsies); brad (Making Memories); Misc: Century Gothic and Steelfish fonts, pen

it's an honor

While my birthday celebration wasn't anything elaborate, what was important to my family was that there was a celebration. Thus, I put my camera in my purse and hauled it out during a lull. I journaled small details that both explain the photos and add humor. Decorative dingbats and minimal journaling give a menu-like look to this restaurant outing.

Supplies: Cardstock (Prism); patterned paper (My Mind's Eye); chipboard (Fancy Pants); letter stickers (Martha Stewart, Mustard Moon); flowers (Prima); brad (Autumn Leaves); Misc: Fontin Sans font, acrylic paint, ribbon

one-of-a-kind celebration

Annual get-togethers can become much-loved celebrations and deserve to be scrapped as such. My mom and her sisters gather every summer for what they call "The Hen Party," doing crafts, going shopping, playing cards and dominoes, and even dressing alike some days. There are so many fireworks between the five of them, it's like the Fourth of July.

Supplies: Cardstock (Prism); patterned paper (Crate Paper); chipboard heart, paper flower, rub-ons (Heidi Grace); decorative tape (Heidi Swapp); digital journaling block, patterned paper, ribbon and stamp by Sande Krieger (Two Peas in a Bucket); digital stitches by Tia Bennett (Two Peas in a Bucket); Misc: ClassizismAntqua font, button, ribbon

scrap the forest and the trees

Big events mean big guest lists. Choose photos of both the crowd and individual people at your next big event as Sharyn did here. She's got a layout that really conveys the spirit of this rainy Sunday School picnic, an event she's been going to since she was a child.

Supplies: Cardstock; letters (Making Memories); rub-ons (Hambly); number stickers (7gypsies); Misc: Credit Valley font

Art created by Sharyn Tormanen

prop it up

Every celebration has its own accoutrements. Ask your photo subjects to get theirs front and center so that your photos convey as much about an event as possible. The pansies and "Stop Global Warming" signs the kids collected at this Earth Day event add detail while contributing to the layout's tone. Owl and flower motifs, along with the colors of the sky and grass, complete the Earth Day look.

Supplies: Cardstock (Prism); patterned paper (Sassafras Lass); letter stickers, plastic and felt accents (American Crafts); digital quote block by Sande Krieger (Two Peas in a Bucket); Misc: Pigiarniq font

Each family has its own rhythm of preparing for and celebrating a holiday.
Keep this in mind when you're planning your holiday pages so that you can record preparations,
preholiday outings and the actual day in a way that works best for your photos.

at its essence

Think about what activity or image evokes the absolute essence of a holiday you
celebrate. With Hanukkah in our home, it's the daily anticipation of sundown and
the reverence with which we light the menorah that's at the heart of this holiday.
This is preserved with photographs from three different nights and journaling
about this time.

There is such a lovely sense of anticipation each late afternoon of Hannukah. The boys love so many little things: watching for sundown, recalling which night it is and how many candles are needed, filling the menorah, the actual lighting of the candles and, finally, saying the prayer with their Dad. 2006

Supplies: Cardstock (Prism); patterned paper (My Mind's Eye); letter stickers (Making Memories); rhinestones (Darice, Heidi Swapp, My Mind's Eye); rub-ons (American Crafts); digital flourish by Anna Aspnes (Designer Digitals); digital dot accent by Sande Kreiger (Two Peas in a Bucket); Misc: Pigiarniq font

cut from the same cloth

"Egg Hunt" and "Sweet Morning," below, are both from the same Easter weekend. Coordinated products and similar color schemes tie the two pages together. Other ways to unite a series of pages include: using the same layout design, positioning one element (such as the title) in a consistent spot, and using the same type treatment (such as letter stickers, chipboard letters or fonts) on each page.

Supplies: Image editing software (Adobe); digital papers and ribbon by Summer Simmons (Sugar Giggles); flower sticker, paper by Tia Bennett (Two Peas in a Bucket); Misc: Desyrel and Will & Grace fonts

pre-party shots

Take photos of decorations and gifts before a holiday celebration. These photos trigger different memories than those of people and activities. Enlarge one photo of the decorative elements. Print the rest and trim them to a common height or width. This trimming allows you to treat the supporting photos as a block for mounting and arranging, resulting in a page the conveys the spirit of the event as well as clearly telling the story.

Supplies: Image editing software (Adobe); embellishments, patterned paper (Sugar Giggles); textured paper by Andrea Burns (Digi Chick); torn edge (Digital Paper Tearing); Misc: Desyrel, Dream Orphans and Sweetheart Script fonts

what's your motif?

Use motifs and colors that are strongly associated with the holiday you are scrapping to make it easy for the viewer to enter into your page. The red Swiss polka dots and heart embellishments leave no doubt as to what's being celebrated and provide the perfect backdrop for Betsy's daughter's activities—and cute face!

Art created by Betsy Veldman

Supplies: Cardstock (Die Cuts With A View); die-cut shapes, patterned paper (Sassafras Lass); letter stickers (Mustard Moon); brads (Creative Impressions)

before the celebration

Think about the traditions you have in preparing for a holiday. For this page, I took photos of the constants in our Passover preparations: the standards on our grocery list, our go-to Passover cookbook, and the parsnips and carrots that we use to make broth for our matzo balls. Finally, I included a shot of the boys arranging flowers for the table—a tradition they may someday outgrow, but one I hope they will always remember.

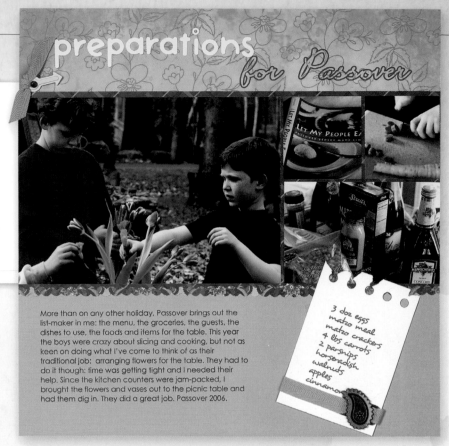

More than on any other holiday, Passover brings out the list-maker in me: the menu, the groceries, the guests, the dishes to use, the foods and items for the table. This year the boys were crazy about slicing and cooking, but not as keen on doing what I've come to think of as their traditional job: arranging flowers for the table. They had to do it though: time was getting tight and I needed their help. Since the kitchen counters were jam-packed, I brought the flowers and vases out to the picnic table and had them dig in. They did a great job. Passover 2006.

Supplies: Cardstock (Bazzill); patterned paper (A2Z); letter stickers (KI Memories); photo turn (7gypsies); ribbon slide (Maya Road); Misc: CBX Heber, Century Gothic and Desyrel fonts, brad, twill

the whole gang

While I've never been a big fan of Halloween, my children *love* it. They plan for it months in advance. They remember all their past costumes as well as those of the neighborhood kids they trick-or-treat with. I took many more shots than I've included on this two-page layout, but this is all my kids need to remember this particular Halloween: one group shot and close-ups of the gang.

Supplies: Cardstock (Prism); patterned paper (Crate Paper); epoxy stickers (American Traditional); metal accent (Pressed Petals); plastic accents (American Crafts); rub-ons (Heidi Grace); Misc: Hannibal Lechter and Pigiarnig fonts, buttons, ribbon, thread

Pages that chronicle your travels allow you to relive the trip even when you're back home. Photos, memorabilia, facts and journaling impressions are all part of the package. And just as important as your far-ranging travels are those closer to home: day trips, outings with friends, local fairs and afternoons at the museum with friends and family.

sensual journaling

Consider your entire surroundings and give your pages even more power with detailed journaling. Betsy describes colors, temperatures, lighting and details about fish and water that evoke the feeling of being in an underwater tunnel. Not only are the words themselves evocative, but her treatment of the type—curved, on a black background, with several words in color—enhances their effect.

You guys loved visiting the aquarium at the Omaha Zoo. It was like entering a whole different world. The dark building was a calm, cool relief from the steamy July weather. You enjoyed watching the colorful fish swim around in their peaceful, blue water worlds. We walked through a tunnel that made us feel as if we were strolling through the ocean with sharks and stingrays swimming around us. It was definitely a highlight of the trip. July 3, 2006

Supplies: Cardstock (Bazzill); patterned paper (Die Cuts With A View, Dream Street, My Mind's Eye); letter stickers (American Crafts); rub-ons (Die Cuts With A View)

Art created by Betsy Veldman

impulse to SOAr

The boys in our house are fascinated by flight: by how it happens and who does it and in what they do it. We have baskets full of paper airplanes and tubs full of die-cast airplanes. We speak frequently of Orville and Wilbur, and . . . if there is a flight museum in our path, we stop. Joshua recently told me his career plans are to repair and fly airplanes -- and then I found out that Isaac no longer wants to play professional football; he wants to fly, too.
    Though I have never had a strong interest in flight, I totally get this: it is what astounds and compels them -- and we all need something like that in our lives. Museum of Flight, Seattle. 06 05.

SIEZE THE DAY

why we go there

This was one stop on our Seattle vacation, and I took a different approach with this page than I did with others from this trip. Rather than telling the details of what we saw, I journaled about my sons' love of this kind of museum. Their fascination goes deeper than an interest in the machinery of the planes. They love the history behind the planes and, even more, they love the idea of flight. In support of my objective with this page, I chose the statue of the boy with a toy plane as my focal point and used part of a Helen Keller quote for the title.

Supplies: Cardstock (Bazzill); patterned paper (Autumn Leaves, KI Memories); chipboard letters (Heidi Swapp); acrylic letters (Jo-Ann); sticker accent (7gypsies); Misc: Frutiger font, ink

but what did you do there?

Sharyn has been coming to this balloon festval since she was a child. Several years ago she stopped journaling about the real meat of the event and concentrated on scrapping the gorgeous pictures because, she thought, it's the same story every year. Looking at those pages later, she realized how much detail was missing and so this year used the photos to support extensive journaling.

Supplies: Cardstock (Bazzill); tag (7gypsies); Misc: Perpetua font, brads

CANDIDS

I look forward to this weekend every year, and now the kids are old enough that they do also.
I remember coming out to the balloon festival when I was a kid, we'd come with the family and watch the balloons take off. I never dreamed, at that time, that I'd live in the very town that the festival is in, it seemed so far away when I was young. Now we live here and enjoy it to the hilt. How much we participate is directly related to the temperature and humidity – or how pregnant I might be or how young the baby is, but we do participate. Our favorite events are the sidewalk art downtown along with all the extra shows – the dog costume show, for example. And yard sales...we can always count on there being a lot of yard sales along our route.
Our route. Yes. We walk. From the school to our home is about 2.5 – 3 miles and we walk it multiple times during this 3 day period. Thank goodness for the Burley! This year found us walking back and forth to the school all 3 days. Did I mention that Greg is never home for balloon festival? As luck would have it, it falls on the exact same

weekend as the St. Ignace car cruise, and he won't miss that, even for balloons. So we trudge, the kids and I – we watch at least one launch, we visit the craft vendors, we enjoy some greasy fair food, this year was the first time we really participated in the rides...I usually skimp out on that but with the two bigs able to ride together, it was easier this year. One thing we never miss is the balloon glow. It takes place at dusk on Saturday night and to me is even more enjoyable than fireworks. The colors are remarkable and the weather is almost always cooperative. And we walk home thru the traffic, crowds and moonlight madness and talk about our favorite parts of the day. And the next morning, I wake up at 6am and sit out on the deck with my vanilla cappuccino in hopes of seeing the balloons flying overhead on their way in.
There's a chance that this may have been our Al's last year as he's finally reached the age where he can go with the boys to St. Ignace if he chooses. I wonder what he'll choose.......

June 24-26 2006
XXII Michigan Challenge

Art created by Sharyn Tormanen

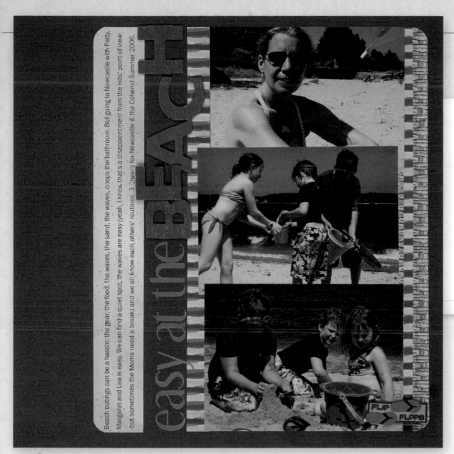

Beach outings can be a hassle: the gear, the food, the waves, the sand, the waves, o-ops the bathroom. But going to Newcastle with Patty, Margaret and Lea is easy. We can find a quiet spot, the waves are easy (yeah, I know, that's a disappointment from the kids' point of view--but sometimes the Moms need a break) and we all know each others' routines. 3 Cheers for Newcastle & the Cohens! Summer 2006.

easy at the BEACH

who else is going to be there?

Local outings are often driven as much by wanting to do something with friends as by the desire to be at a particular location. That's how it is for us when we make our frequent visits to Newcastle Beach with the Cohens. While "Easy at the Beach" has photos from one particular beach outing, the journaling tells about the nature of our outings when we're with these girls. Remember to talk about the constants that keep bringing you back to your favorite local destinations.

Supplies: Cardstock, patterned paper, sandal accent (American Traditional); letter stickers (Arctic Frog); chipboard letters (We R Memory Keepers); Misc: ITC Franklin Gothic font

memorabilia matters

The inclusion of an information-filled brochure from this outing lets me concentrate on personal journaling on this photo-filled layout. Small artifacts are also wonderful memory triggers if you can fit them in. The small pieces of mica on this page are sealed under the lid to a small tin.

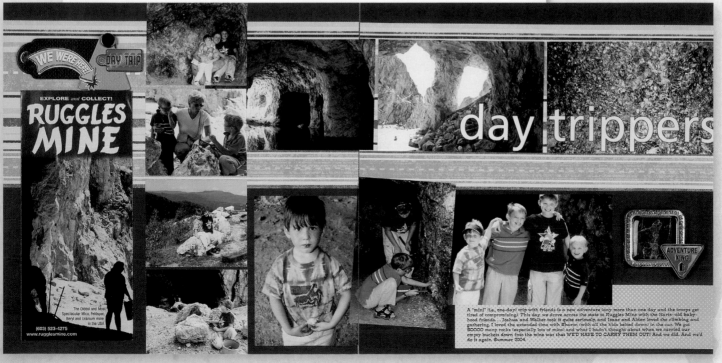

Supplies: Cardstock, patterned paper, travel accents (American Traditional); chipboard (Pressed Petals); box lid (Maya Road); Misc: Expo and Frutiger fonts, brads, mica

How Kim Kesti Gets Events Scrapped

What Kim gets onto her scrapbook pages is driven by the photos she takes, and she makes every effort to take a lot of them—up close, far back, straight on and at different angles. This way she ensures she's got a multitude to choose from when she goes to make her pages.

Kim likes to get a lot of photos on the page, and she doesn't often make enlargements, unless there's a photo that really catches her eye—check out "Summer Yum" on page 45. While Kim doesn't often enlarge her photos, what she does is print wallet-sized, 2" x 3" (5cm x 8cm), photos. They're a great size for her to "pop" onto her multi-photo pages, especially when she's scrapping in an 8.5" x 11" (22cm x 28cm) format like "Ashley's Wedding Shower" on the next page.

Kim's design preferences tend toward the simple, with every element supporting the page's subject and meaning. Again, the photos drive what Kim does with color and style. Check out the license plate on "Taxi" and the southwestern-styled sun on "See Santa Fe" (both on page 44). Kim's so in tune with what the photos call for, she's absolutely willing to step outside of her clean-lined comfort zone when necessary, as illustrated on her daughter's birthday layout on the next page through the use of fairy wings and lots of hand doodling.

When I'm working on event pages, I've found Kim to be a great inspiration. Her pages provide great examples of using the right photos, getting many of them on a page and really capturing the spirit of any celebration.

Supplies: Cardstock (Prism); patterned paper, rub-ons, stickers (Daisy D's); buttons (Autumn Leaves); Misc: floss, pen

all about whimsy

This page featuring Kim's daughter's birthday shows that you can scrap more than details—you can convey a whole mood and tone to match your celebration. Aiming for a light and whimsical feel, Kim used a patterned paper that matched the party's theme, included charming little buttons, and added hand doodling to the distressed rub-ons and stickers.

Art created by Kim Kesti

color my world

Kim's philosophy about scrapping wedding and baby showers is: "Don't fight it," meaning go ahead and use the colors of the party, and the scrapping will be much easier. Here, scalloped teal paper backs up a two-page layout and works to tie the two pages together.

Supplies: Cardstock (Bazzill); patterned paper (Creative Imaginations); letter stickers (American Crafts); ribbon (Michaels); rub-ons (Luxe Designs); stamp (7gypsies); stickers (Heidi Swapp); Misc: ink, pen

Art created by Kim Kesti

whirlwind tour?

Do you ever think "why bother?" when you're spending a very brief time in a new place? Well don't! Take your camera along and photograph something. When Kim had only 24 hours in New York City and spent a good chunk of that time eating an Italian dinner outdoors, it was taxis that she saw and taxis that she photographed. This trip with her friend isn't going to be left out of the album, and her journaling conveys her excitement and discoveries about a first-time trip to the Big Apple.

new york and taxis. the two just seem to go together in my mind. i was able to make my first trip to the big city on labor day weekend, 2005. i admit to being a little nervous, but i was super excited at the same time. allison landy and i were chauffered to our hotel from connecticut, after attending a business meeting there for two days. we only had approximately 24 hours in the city, so we checked into the upper east side marriott, dropped our bags and hit the streets. we enjoyed an italian dinner sitting outside while watching the people and the traffic zip by. it was amazing! i never knew there were so many taxis in existence. so, naturally i had to do what any good tourist would, and snap about a zillion photos. so, here s my nod to new york and it s wonderful taxis. taxi!

Supplies: Cardstock (Bazzill); mailbox letters, rub-ons (Making Memories); sticker (7gypsies); bookplate (BasicGrey); license plate (Creative Imaginations); Misc: Airstrip Four font

Art created by Kim Kesti

show and tell

You may think you'll never forget the details of travel sights that awe you. But just to make sure, take time to journal about them, including names and local significance as Kim does here.

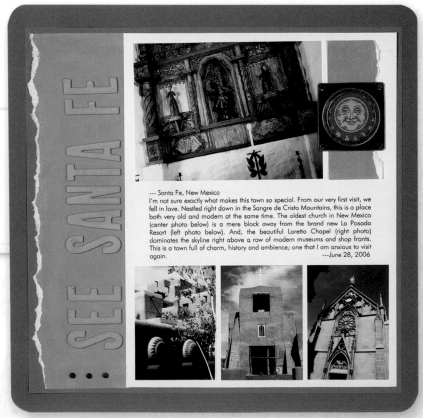

SEE SANTA FE

--- Santa Fe, New Mexico
I'm not sure exactly what makes this town so special. From our very first visit, we fell in love. Nestled right down in the Sangre de Cristo Mountains, this is a place both very old and modern at the same time. The oldest church in New Mexico (center photo below) is a mere block away from the brand new La Posada Resort (left photo below). And, the beautiful Loretto Chapel (right photo) dominates the skyline right above a row of modern museums and shop fronts. This is a town full of charm, history and ambience; one that I am anxious to visit again.
---June 28, 2006

Supplies: Cardstock (Bazzill); chipboard letters (American Crafts); frame (Li'l Davis); stamp (PSX); Misc: acrylic paint, brads, ink

Art created by Kim Kesti

Art created by Kim Kesti

the big picture

After scrapping many of her Hawaiian vacation photos, Kim had a pile of shots that she really liked but that didn't fit with any other pages. She cropped each photo to the same size and lined them to get a big-picture layout that encapsulates her "trip of a lifetime" to Maui.

Supplies: Cardstock (Bazzill); patterned paper (7gypsies); decorative tape, title letters (Heidi Swapp)

celebrate annual rituals

Every year Harry helps his grandfather make ice cream. While some of us may not think of this as an event, Harry certainly does. Photographing all the details of a personal event from beginning to end results in a great record.

Supplies: Cardstock (Bazzill); patterned paper (Scrapworks); chipboard and plastic letters (Heidi Swapp); buttons (Doodlebug); rub-on (Hambly); Misc: acrylic paint, brads

Art created by Kim Kesti

DATE	SUBJECT/OCCASION	PLACE	COMMENTS

Chapter 3
Get Everyday Life Scrapped

This chapter is about scrapping your around-the-house, hanging-out-with-friends, recording-the-garden's-progress kind of photos.

This group of photos can be the hardest to "get your arms around." They aren't associated with a particular holiday or event; they tend to be broad in scope; and they don't always lend themselves to chronological organization. This chapter offers an easy approach for getting everyday life photos into groupings that will translate well to scrapbook pages.

Organizing Everyday Life Photos

as your photos arrive	File non-event, everyday life photos in a digital folder or index-tabbed section of your photo box called ''YYYY MM At Home'' * yyyy=year, mm=month
periodically (weekly, monthly, quarterly or whatever matches the volume of your photos and the rhythm of your scrapbooking)	Go through your ''Everyday Photos'' to: 1) Break out stories or mini-events (such as making a snowman or a neighborhood squirt-gun fight). Give each of these stories a spot on your plan, and either label them digitally or give them their own tabbed index card section. This makes them easy to grab when you want to scrap. 2) File the rest of your everyday photos by category. Use digital folders or index-tabbed sections of your photo box that fit your life and family. As the folders grow, you can create collection layouts (see Chapter 4) with them. Examples of categories: outdoor play, spending time with Grandma and Grandpa, quality time between siblings, hanging out around the house, hanging out with friends . . .

summer
afternoon

CHILDHOOD

We are nesters and schleppers--even when we're just going to the back yard. Inside of the pop-up beach tent I can see an old baby blanket and Isaac's stuffed Panda and, Joshua, you probably brought that big old wind gun out. I'm sure there are more pillows and a deck of cards in there. Water bottles, bug spray, & my diet coke can are scattered on the grass. On this afternoon, I sat in my green chair and read Artemis Fowl while you two lazed. Perfect & Typical. 2006.

this is how we do it

What are the activities in your life that you take for granted? Sure, I've got lots of photos from our summer beach outings, but not so many of our more frequent summer activity of setting up the beach tent in the yard, hauling out some pillows and snacks, and settling in to read. Looking at these photos just a year after taking them, I immediately wanted to get the story of this afternoon on the page to record just how we do it.

Supplies: Cardstock (Bazzill); patterned paper (Imaginisce); letter stickers (Arctic Frog); word sticker (KI Memories); die-cut letters (Provo Craft); photo turns (7gypsies); Misc: ITC Franklin Gothic font, brad

stay back

Use your camera's zoom feature to take photos from a distance and avoid disrupting the very activity you want to capture. And don't just shoot—listen, too. Using this technique I was able to figure out that Chris was in charge of this neighborhood play and understand the ground rules they were using (as well as the care they were taking not to "poke an eye out")—all information that went into the page's journaling.

Supplies: Cardstock (American Traditional, Prism); patterned paper, sticker (American Traditional); crop marks by Katie Pertiet (Designer Digitals); Misc: Palatino Linotype and Steelfish fonts, chipboard, ink

carry a BIG STICK

When I stepped out my door on a fall afternoon and saw this sight, it didn't scare me. Rather, the boys' elegance and care impressed me.

Chris had developed a new stick fighting technique, and he was training the rest of the boys in the neighborhood. I can't say how it works, but there are ways to gain points and lose points, and no one should get hit hard, but to score a point you do need to make contact.

These boys, ranging from 6 to 10 years old, were taking each other on and playing according to their own code of conduct and having a great time. {and no one poked an eye out}. Fall 06.

BE YOURSELF

As you're thinking about how to creatively present everyday life photos, consider these approaches:

* Preserve a particular story or incident with representative photos and journaling that tell what happened.

* Record a routine with photos from one occurrence and journaling that tells about how this routine fits into your life.

* Create a record of your family members' activities around organized groups, like school, church, sports and clubs.

* Put many candids on the page around a theme, i.e., your daughter around the house, your son with his friends.

I love "garbage night" in the spring and summer. I love the irony of garbage bringing us together with our neighbors. Early Sunday evening, we pull wheeled garbage cans up our long driveways to the cul-de-sac. "Cans this week? Or boxes." "Boxes. How was your weekend?" Then the kids bring up the recycling in their wagon--"do we have to?"--slowly, yakking the whole way, finally telling me the stuff I've been asking about all week. They unload & Isaac hops in the wagon & demands a ride. It ends up taking a good half-hour for them to play their way back home--just in time for Sunday night baths. And that's another garbage night well spent. 2006.

it's not a one-time thing

Show one time in photos, but tell about the many times in your journaling. The photos here show one Sunday evening of hauling out the trash to the curbside, but the journaling talks about "Garbage Night's" regular place in our lives. I record my own feeling of irony at connecting with neighbors over our trash cans as well as the nature of the boys' yakking and the subsequent Sunday night baths.

Supplies: Cardstock (Bazzill); patterned paper (K&Co., Urban Lily); chipboard letters (Li'l Davis); letter stickers (Arctic Frog); chipboard star (Magistical Memories); die-cut flower (QuicKutz); metallic floss (DMC); ribbon (Michaels); buttons (Autumn Leaves); Misc: Centaur and Century Gothic fonts, concho, paint

If you want to be sure you're capturing the real life that's going on around you,
get in the habit of:

* keeping your batteries charged
* keeping your digital cards clean or film on-hand
* keeping your camera out and handy

Consider taking a month to challenge yourself to take a photo a day (of course, you can take more).
You'll find yourself seeing your homelife in a new way, and you'll make the effort to grab the
camera when something simple happens, like your child showing you a school project he's just
brought home or balancing a spoon on his nose.

before, during & after

When you want to remember an event you
don't have much access to, try the before-
during-after approach I used to scrap this
campout. I took a photo of the group in the
evening right before they retired on the front
steps of the camper. During one of my check-
up visits, I got a shot of all of them inside the
camper, and then the next morning, a photo of
them with messy hair at the front door of the
house with the rising sun in the background.

Supplies: Cardstock (Bazzill); patterned paper, square sticker (7gypsies);
chipboard letters (Heidi Swapp); letter stickers (Li'l Davis); word stickers
(Making Memories); metal square (Pressed Petals); Misc: Palatino Linotype
font, chipboard square, photo corners

The situations around everyday life photos are often small stories and that can mean remembering them later may not be easy. To help with this, get in the habit of journaling in a way that works for you. This can include a bulleted list of items, brief notes, as well as full journal entries.

These writings could go:
* on an oversized calendar
* on sticky notes or index cards that you store with your photos
* in a journal
* on a blog for your extended family

Find an approach that works best for you. It may not be possible to document every detail, but when it comes time to scrap you will value the tidbits you were able to capture through journaling.

NOT A CLOUD in the sky

Sunday afternoon. I'm reading on the screened porch and the kids are playing with neighbors at The Big Rock. Isaac comes down, goes inside, comes back out with an umbrella and returns with it to The Big Rock. Next door, I see Aiden going up the driveway with an umbrella. Huh? It's sunny! I've got to see what's going on and so I venture up to The Big Rock where 8 kids are under 8 umbrellas . . . . . reading. They wanted shade. And now they're thinking a snack would be good. Absolutely. A snack would be good.

how it went down

Write the story in a tone your family will love. The journaling here is written in the present tense. The storyteller is in the dark for a while, trying to figure out just what the children—who turn out to be very clever—are up to. While it's a simple story, my kids think it's really funny, and I know years from now they will look back and laugh.

Supplies: Cardstock (Bazzill); patterned paper (Chatterbox, Urban Lily); metal letters (Jo-Ann); fabric tabs (Scrapworks); ribbon (May Arts); rickrack (Wrights); brads; oval plate (Making Memories); decorative border punch (Fiskars); Misc: Bernard Modern BT and CAC Pinafore fonts, brads

When cropping and placing photos of people onto everyday life pages, the direction in which your subject is looking is the direction in which the viewer's eye will go. Follow these basic tips for an eye-pleasing design.

* Consciously crop and place photos of people to guide the viewer's eye into your page rather than off of the page.

* Position a photo of a subject looking to the right toward the left side of the page (and vice versa). Also, be aware of subjects and their activities implying downward or upward movement and position accordingly. A photo of a subject looking down would be better placed toward the top rather than the bottom where it would guide the eye off the page.

* When a subject is looking straight ahead, use cropping to direct the eye. Crop so that your subject sits more on the left side of the photo so viewer's eye will move to the right (and vice versa).

collage it

Collage several uncropped photos across two pages for an energetic layout that can be pulled together quickly and easily. During this snowball fight, I snapped photos of everyone from varying angles and distances. When it came time to scrap, I chose photos that all had a portrait orientation to give this layout form.

Supplies: Cardstock (Prism); patterned paper (BasicGrey); plastic letters (Heidi Swapp); rub-on letters (Royal & Langnickel); photo turns (7gypsies); Misc: AL Uncle Charles font, brads

Families have their own culture — it's like a secret club. When you scrapbook pages of the stories, characteristics and routines of your family, you'll have a record of how that culture arises and evolves. You'll also have some pages that are really fun to revisit.

illustrated stories

Tell the stories of everyday events with one enlarged photo that includes your character in a world full of context. This photo shows my son looking down at me from his bunk bed. The pictures on his wall have been there the last couple of years, but there will come a time when he'll change them—maybe even tack up posters! Other details he and I both love seeing are his bear with the dirty head and the Mardi Gras necklaces and Hawaiian lei that hang on his bedpost. He's the protagonist of the story, and this is his world.

Supplies: Cardstock (Bazzill); patterned paper (7gypsies, K&Co., We R Memory Keepers); chipboard (Technique Tuesday); stickers (Li'l Davis); rub-ons (7gypsies, Creative Imaginations, Fancy Pants); ribbon (Offray); transparency; letter brads (K&Co.); Misc: Centaur font, ink, staples

the story behind the story

While you're writing down the details of what happened, be sure to tell why it matters. Tell what makes it particularly story-worthy. In "Secrets of the Cat Whisperer," I wrote about my son's patient pursuit of some wild kittens and, at the same time, of how he often gives up difficult pursuits because of his fear of failing.

Supplies: Image editing software (Adobe); papers by Summer Simmons (Sugar Giggles); Misc: Georgia, Jane Austen, Port Credit and Suzy's Hand fonts

secrets of the

be patient

know where to look

approach low

make a toy

CAT whisperer

Isaac, It's always interesting to see what you're willing to work on. While many challenges send you running because you don't like failing or being wrong, cats are worth the risk. The new kittens at Grandma and Grandpa's had never been handled and they went running when anyone came near. You worked at getting close for hours, taking several approaches until, finally, you did get to pet a couple. You were very satisfied.

the small stuff

When the kids are doing something that makes you say, "Wait! Let me get the camera," come back prepared to take photos not only of them, but of all the little things that will clarify and enhance the story when you look at the photos years later. Here, photos show just how my sons "harvested" ice from leaves and made an ice salad, as well as how they looked and what they were doing with those ice leaves.

when life gives you ice, make ice salad

One day right after an ice storm, Joshua said he was going out to "harvest ice," and I told him the ice in icicles rolls off roof shingles and has chemicals in it. And he and Isaac went out. An hour later, he & Isaac came in and said "Do you want to do a layout of our ice salad?" (Isn't nice how they look out for my interests? ;)) Of course I went out and they shared their salad AND their recipe with me.
ICE SALAD
1) slide ice off from leaves so that it retains the leaf impression; 2) Put gently in a bowl; 3) Sprinkle with snow dressing if desired. 4) Enjoy!

Supplies: Cardstock (Bazzill); patterned paper (American Traditional, Creative Imaginations, KI Memories, Scenic Route); letter stickers (Li'l Davis); die-cut letters and shape (Provo Craft); fruit accent (American Traditional); Misc: CBX Heber and Roman Serif fonts, brads, chipboard, ink

all the world's a stage

Stage a shoot of something you take for granted. Several days a week, I hear the clomp of my husband's bike shoes across the kitchen floor and out through the mudroom. The door opens and closes, and he's gone for one to two hours. I recently realized I had no photos of this activity that is so central to my husband's life, so I put it right with this photo shoot.

miles to go
{and promises to keep}

How does it feel to set an ambitious and difficult goal and more than meet it? Over this last summer & into the fall you logged more than 2,200 miles on your bike--more than on your car! You rode everywhere: work, meetings, errands for me, volunteering at school, and even the mall. The results I can see from this are more than increased fitness. I see your satisfaction in having done this for yourself and in providing a great model for all of us. The most surprising by-product, though, is that you've increased your ability exist in silence -- without the stereo, radio, book in your hand. Way, to go, Neil! XO Debbie

Supplies: Cardstock (Bazzill); chipboard letters (Heidi Swapp); Misc: Palatino Linotype font

Time spent with friends and extended family will yield stories and mini events that you'll want on your pages. These pages make a record of who you spent time with and how that time was spent—something that will change year-to-year. When these pages are viewed over time, they'll provide a portrait of your social and familial relationships.

while it's fresh

I love that feeling I have when I've taken some great photos of a memorable outing with family. Usually, I flag the photos, make a few notes and think about what a great layout it will make. Unfortunately, a lot of those stories still haven't made it onto the page. Not this one, though. A few days after this hike, I put together a quick digital page with photos all cropped to the same size and the emphasis on the story. Sometimes you just need to throw the plan away and scrap what compels you at the moment.

is the shortcut

There was a point about 45 minutes into the hike when Mark--who was telling stories I'd never heard about these once-familiar landmarks (WWII munitions? Old trapper's cabin?)-- actually said, "We need to get moving. We're not even halfway there." Oh, halfway-scmalfway. We've got plenty of time. But time does not equate to energy, and things can get especially bad if your children have inherited your own tendency to express every feeling (i.e., I'm tired; I'm hungry; My feet hurt.) We did make it to the stone quarry and enjoyed seeing it, but then someone said, "How far is it back?" Mark said, "We'll take the shortcut." Isaac said, "Is it shorter?" And we laughed. Ah, the wisdom of children. July 2007.

shorter?

while that's unclear, we do know it's wetter.

Supplies: Image editing software (Adobe); paper by Katie Pertiet (Designer Digitals); Misc: Antique Type, Century Gothic, GeoSlab and Impact fonts

get the job done

When Kim's sons and their friends reworked an old moped, she got photos that convey both how they did the job and their excitement over the project. To share this kind of a record with the whole gang, use a scanner and software to get a digital copy of the layout that you can print many times.

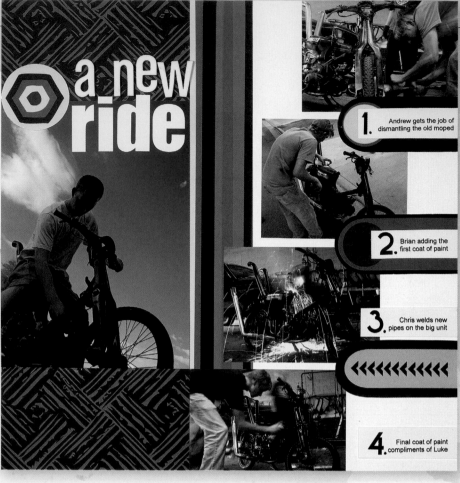

Supplies: Cardstock (Bazzill); patterned paper (Tinkering Ink); letter stickers (American Crafts); rub-on (Luxe Designs); stickers (Reminisce); Misc: Arial font

Art created by Kim Kesti

start at the very beginning

Just like the stories we read or the movies we watch, each of our everyday stories has a beginning, a middle and an end. The photos in "Moving In" are arranged in a horizontal strip to convey a chronology. When my friend, Jill, moved into her new massage studio, another friend and I were there to help out. The viewer's eye begins with the photo of the building's exterior at the far left and proceeds across, through the toilet cleaning and spackling, to end up with a final hug between friends.

Supplies: Cardstock (Bazzill, Prism); patterned paper (Heidi Grace); letter stickers (American Crafts, KI Memories); metal accents, pin, square button (Heidi Grace); transparency (My Mind's Eye); label plate (Li'l Davis); rhinestone; photo turn (Creative Impressions); Misc: Palatino Linotype font, buttons, floss, pen, rhinestone

bookends

When you have lots of photos and busy backgrounds, create one or two focal photos using image-editing software. Here, I zoomed in on the detail of my mom with the hose to begin this story. Several busy photos lie between this shot and another close-up—this one of the kids' grassy feet. These two detailed photos "bookend" the other busy but fun shots to convey what is going on.

Supplies: Cardstock (Bazzill, Prism); patterned paper (A2Z); die-cut flowers, heart and letters (Provo Craft); Misc: Palatino Linotype font, brads, ink

cutting it close

Want to fit eight 4" x 6" (10cm x 15cm) photos on one page? Try this: Crop, abut and bleed. I have rarely had a 4" x 6" (10cm x 15cm) photo that couldn't be trimmed down—and some close cropping can yield dynamic results. Crop your photos to 3" x 5" (8cm x 13cm) then line them up side by side with no gutters and let them bleed off the edge of your page. A 2" (5cm) strip of cardstock through the middle provides a spot for title and journaling, and you've scrapped it in no time. Notice that the photo of my niece in purple was actually a landscape photo that I turned portrait. Like this design? Turn it 90° and do it again with landscape photos.

Supplies: Cardstock (Prism); letter stickers (American Crafts, American Traditional); number stickers (Li'l Davis); chipboard arrow (American Crafts); decorative tape (7gypsies); cord (Jo-Ann); digital brush by Tia Bennett (Designer Digitals); Misc: Weathered Fence font

When you're taking and scrapping everyday life photos, don't forget about the organized activities and groups with which your family is involved. These groups include school, church, sports and clubs. Depending on the volume of photos you have, these layouts often make good collection layouts (see Chapter 4).

what's your motif?

When your photos and subject are closely associated with an image—like a big yellow school bus—use that to the max. Betsy threaded the school bus motif throughout this layout: naming it in the title, showing it in the photos and even using a yellow background with bus-like black stripes to create an energetic page.

You had an awesome first day of kindergarten! You were so excited for your first ride on the school bus. We brought you in the morning, so you had to wait until school was over for the big moment! The look of determination on your face as you got off the bus was priceless! Oh, and we decided no kids were going to mess with you on your first day... you went to school with a great big black eye from a bike accident a few days before school started!

Supplies: Cardstock (Die Cuts With A View); patterned paper (American Crafts, KI Memories, My Mind's Eye); ribbon (KI Memories); letter stickers (American Crafts); sticker accents (7gypsies); metal clip (Making Memories); digital journal tag by Michelle Underwood (Scrapbook Bytes); chipboard stars (Pressed Petals)

Art created by Betsy Veldman

This layout from one game serves as a great trigger for our whole family for this particular baseball season. Alongside it I'll put a pocket page with photos of the team and a few other action shots.

Supplies: Cardstock (Prism); patterned paper (Urban Lily); letter stickers (American Crafts); chipboard accents (Fancy Pants, Li'l Davis, Magistical Memories); leather strips (Li'l Davis); pen (Sakura); Misc: acrylic paint

let's go clubbin'

At least once a year, I take photos of my knitting group. It's not really planned, but I have my camera in my bag most of the time so that I can take photos when it seems right. On this night, we were learning how to needle felt, and someone said, "We should get some photos of this." No problem. I love having layouts of my "clubs" in the albums alongside all my kids' organized activities.

Supplies: Cardstock (Prism); felt flowers, letter stickers, patterned paper, plastic shapes (American Crafts); felt (CPE); Misc: Beffle and Pigiarnig fonts, brads

How Sharyn Jormanen Gets Everyday Life Scrapped

Sharyn remembers a friend with older children telling her that she should be sure to record those ever-changing, but oh-so-common, things like the full cereal bowls right before the kids come stampeding down the stairs in the morning. Sharyn has taken that to heart and the subjects she scrapbooks are driven by conscious decisions to capture what might be taken for granted now—but not in the future.

Take a look at her "Monkey Love" layout on the next page, have your heartstrings tugged, and you'll understand why Sharyn scraps this way. It's like a mini-memoir on the page. This approach means Sharyn is usually photographing what she wants to scrap rather than scrapping what she's photographed.

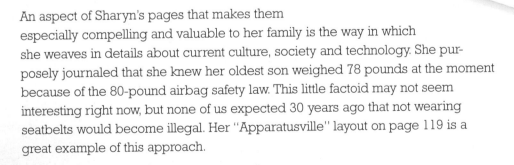

An aspect of Sharyn's pages that makes them especially compelling and valuable to her family is the way in which she weaves in details about current culture, society and technology. She purposely journaled that she knew her oldest son weighed 78 pounds at the moment because of the 80-pound airbag safety law. This little factoid may not seem interesting right now, but none of us expected 30 years ago that not wearing seatbelts would become illegal. Her "Apparatusville" layout on page 119 is a great example of this approach.

Sharyn is an avid blogger, with her daily posts acting as memoir or diary and providing details and inspiration for her pages. When we started working on this book, I mentioned how much I loved her post about the kids on the bed with the clean feet. "Yeah!" she said, "I'm making a page out of it." Witness "What I See" on page 64, and you just might be a convert to Sharyn's approach.

Art created by Sharyn Tormanen

the facts, ma'am

The photos show Sharyn's daughter Wendy with her friends and teacher. The journaling gets the details in that Wendy might not realize or remember later—like the parallels with her older brother's kindergarten experience and the way kindergarten schedules are structured in her community.

Supplies: Patterned paper (Autumn Leaves, Imagination Project); chipboard letter, letter stickers (Making Memories); word sticker (7gypsies); Misc: Garamond font

context is everything

The details Sharyn photographed on a day that her two-year-old endured a separation from his monkey are full of context that makes this page resonate now and in years to come. The sink and the soapsuds as well as the jeans on the line paint a picture not only of this moment but of life as it is lived daily in Sharyn's home now.

Supplies: Cardstock (Bazzill); patterned paper (My Mind's Eye); word stickers (7gypsies); letter stickers (Making Memories); transparent letters (Heidi Swapp); flower and heart accents (Doodlebug); tickets (Jenni Bowlin); transparency (EK Success); Misc: pen

Art created by Sharyn Tormanen

For the Record...

...we do feed this boy. He gets 3 square meals a day the same as the rest of us. He just wants more. If you sit at our table with food, it's guaranteed that within minutes Brian will be there peering over your shoulder with his big blue 'please' puppy dog eyes and with voiceless begging will point from your plate to his mouth. And while some pretend to be he tough, nobody has been able to say no yet.

Art created by Sharyn Tormanen

taking it for granted

Brian's penchant for mooching food from his brother and sister is a regular occurrence in Sharyn's home right now. Realizing that they were beginning to take it for granted, Sharyn took photos and made this page. "It'll just stop one day," says Sharyn, "and I won't recall it again until we look through our books and come across this page, and it'll be, 'Oh, yeah!'"

Supplies: Cardstock (Bazzill); patterned paper (Fontwerks); photo turn, stamps (Technique Tuesday); Misc: Times New Roman font, brad, ink

life unscripted

Sharyn was taking snapshots of her new baby when she realized that all four of her kids were together and not fighting. Right then, she decided to take a group shot on the bed. What she got was much more than she expected. She got photos full of the little details that are powerful memory triggers for a family: her daughter missing teeth, unexpectedly clean feet that mean it's winter, the corduroy quilt and all four kids at this one moment in time.

Supplies: Cardstock (Bazzill); chipboard letters (Heidi Swapp); flower (American Crafts); heart (Doodlebug); Misc: Garamond font

What I See...

4 Kids!

Besides the very first picture of all four Torm-kids together, I see so much more...

I see, *sigh*. I see Allan's hoodie. Again. He wears it every.single.day. It's one of those fights that I've decided just isn't worth it. The shirt underneath is clean, and that's what matters, right? Right??

I see Wendy's jammies. A girl after my own heart, she loves a new pair of jams. She's worn them day and night since she got them – a present from my mom – she knows how to hibernate in the winter!

Ah...and I see by Brian's hands that Wendy left her markers out again. How many times have I told that girl???

And Brian's mismatched jammies – he's not feeling well, poor kid.

I see teeth, or shall I say, I don't see teeth. Wendy's toothless grin cracks me up

And wonders of wonders – I see clean feet. Not hard to tell that this is a photo taken in the dead of winter

And oh....my warm cozy heavy corduroy quilt on top of flannel sheets. I will sleep with those again someday. I will!

A fourth kid. Our Mark. He grabbed everyone's attention when he sneezed

And I see 4 kids. My goodness – I have 4 kids!

Art created by Sharyn Tormanen

Art created by Sharyn Tormanen

more than the obvious

When Sharyn saw these photos, she was struck by her son's hands: active and weathered, nails chewed, bad cuticles, wrinkled from water. She loved how they showed Allan as a boy living a full life. Her layout gives us both the story of him catching a turtle and a portrait of him, as inspired by the state of his hands.

Supplies: Patterned paper (Sandylion); chipboard letters (Heidi Swapp); stamps (Technique Tuesday); rub-ons (Hambly); Misc: ink, pen

photo a day

If you really want to capture regular life, try taking photos every day. The photos on this page were taken over the six days that Sharyn's mom visited right after the birth of Sharyn's fourth child. The result is a page that captures the rhythm of life in Sharyn's house when Grandma is there.

Supplies: Cardstock (Bazzill); patterned paper (Creative Imaginations, Sassafras Lass); acrylic letters (Heidi Swapp); brads, flowers (Queen & Co.); Misc: floss, pen

Art created by Sharyn Tormanen

Chapter 4

Get Collections Scrapped

Collecting related photos that were taken at different times onto one page is a great way to scrap more photos efficiently.

Additionally, when related photos are gathered on the same page you can see the bigger meaning: the forest as well as the trees. This chapter will show you creative ways to showcase a variety of collections. This can include collections of favorite items, featuring a month in review, highlighting photos from an entire school year or tracking a baby's progress from month to month. Flip the page to see all the possibilities for scrapping your collections!

A trend isn't a trend until it's been happening for a while. And you don't always know that a photo belongs in a collection until a few months or years down the road. Here's a method to flag and file your photos, so that when you realize you want to make a collection page, you can find what you need and get it done.

Organizing Photos for Collections

flag	When you are periodically going through the most recent photos you've taken, flag those that don't merit their own page but that you'd like to eventually get into the album with other similarly themed photos. See page 20 for more specifics.
store	File these photos in an acid-free box just for collection photos. Store each themed group of photos behind its own appropriately labeled tabbed index card. Some categories that I keep ongoing include: one for each of my sons with their grandparents, one for each of my sons with their dad, one for each of my sons with their friends, one for each of my sons and particular sports they play, one for home improvement projects, one for shots of me and my husband together.

onesies

I'd flagged each of these photos because I felt they had to go in the album, but I wasn't sure where. None of them are part of a larger event, and none of them are really stellar shots. Together, though, they are a fun portrait of my youngest son at a certain stage in his life. The lesson? Flag and collect those onesies.

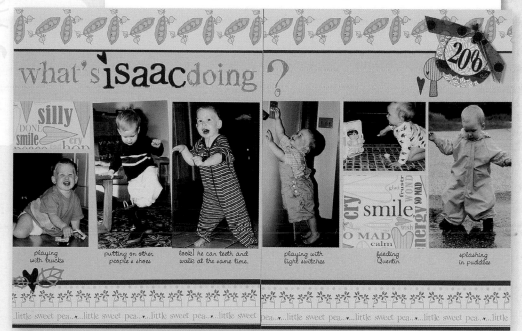

Supplies: Cardstock (Prism); letter stickers, patterned paper, pin, ribbon, rub-ons (Heidi Grace); number stickers (Scrapworks); tags (Martha Stewart); Misc: CAC Pinnafore, Sketchy and Times New Roman fonts

taking stock

As I gathered these photos, I was thinking about the specific whens and wheres of each shot, with the intention of documenting what my husband and I had looked like and done together over the years. When I saw all of the photos gathered, though, they had a power I hadn't expected. They let me look past the small details and really comprehend what fifteen years together add up to.

Supplies: Cardstock (Prism); chipboard butterfly, flower, patterned paper, tags (Prima); plastic letters (Heidi Swapp); fabric tabs (Making Memories); photo turn (Creative Imaginations); eyelet (We R Memory Keepers); die-cut shape (Provo Craft); stamp (Autumn Leaves); pen (Sakura); Misc: Gentium and Pigiarnig fonts, ink, velvet ribbon

Photos: Barbara Hodge

Understanding Collection Pages

Think about the following types of collections as they relate to your life and your photos.

* **Repetitions:** the annual Sunday school picnic, the baseball team photo each year, the first day of school.
* **Changes:** an infant's monthly accomplishments, annual school photos, progress on the yard project.
* **Line-ups:** profiles, outfits, any concrete object you have a collection of that's important to you.
* **Themes:** summer outings, art projects from a certain time period, sibling candids.

they'll do it every time

Are there particular moments when you find yourself taking photos over and over? Looking through photos from past visits to my family, I found that every folder had goodbye shots.

sweet sorrow {what parting is}

Goodbyes in Oxford take a while and have become almost a ceremony. There's the goodbyes to the girls on the last night we're there -- as if we aren't going to see each other in the morning--which we may not. But most times, they come back by or we stop there for additional hugs. It's a lot of hugs. Everybody hugs everybody else. And then there's Grandma and Grandpa and that's when the boys really have a hard time fighting tears. At long last we do leave---with promises that we'll be back soon.

Supplies: Patterned paper, pin, ribbon (Heidi Grace); chipboard (Heidi Grace, Prima); stickers (7gypsies, Heidi Grace, Making Memories); eyelet (We R Memory Keepers); image editing software (Adobe); digital brush (Heather Ann Designs); Misc: Fontin Sans, Geoslab and Scriptina fonts

When flagging and collecting photos, you'll find they are a variety of sizes, formats and styles. Try these approaches to bring order to disparate photos.

* **Look** for opportunities to crop photos to a common height (to line up in a row), a common width (to line up in a column) or a common overall size (to arrange in a grid).

* **Consider** converting some or all of the photos to black and white if there is a great range of color and extra detail that distracts or overwhelms.

* **Select** one photo to feature and enlarge it to act as a focal point with the others as support so that the subject of your page is clear.

modus operandi

Kim took a series of photos of her daughter's current purse and shoe line-up against the same non-distracting background. Notice, also, that her daughter is always wearing denim and that her face isn't included in the photo. All this puts the emphasis right where it belongs: on a supremely fun collection her daughter is going to love looking at now and in twenty years.

Supplies: Cardstock (Bazzill); chipboard (Li'l Davis); rub-on (Scenic Route); die-cut flower (Paper House); rickrack (Wrights); ribbon (American Crafts, May Arts); decorative tape (7gypsies); Misc: Times New Roman font, raffle ticket, shopping bag

Art created by Kim Kesti

Use one of the following approaches, or a combination of the two, for journaling on collection pages.

1. Document the factual details relevant to your collection. Reference "Hand Carved" below and "Little Women" on page 74 to see examples of easy ways to do this.

2. Journal about the greater meaning attached to your collection. For this approach, check out page 114 to see how to use concrete details as a springboard for meaningful journaling.

do tell

This impressive line-up deserves an explanation, and Sharyn provided that in narrative journaling about how her husband got started carving. In addition, she used journaling strips along the bottom to note the date and interesting details about each piece.

This is but just a small portion of Greg's carvings, a good glimpse of what he's done and learned from beginning to now. And I love that it all began with me just happening to meet Stan Bowers doing carvings and book signings at the local bookstore After talking with him for a bit, I took his card and said, "I think my husband might be interested in this" I think I was right. Greg signed up for classes shortly after and never quit!

From left to right: 1) He began with boots and ornaments, 2002/3   2) Fall 2005 he took a 3 day class with Pete LeClair   3) Babushka ladies were very early on   4) Late 2006 – a practice in carving faces

5) His hope is to make a 7 foot Indian someday 6) Two of an assortment of Vikings – he sold at least two others   7) Big Lipped Hounds - My personal favorite and Greg's own pattern 8) Practice for a consignment piece   9)Sailors three – a practice in paints and stains   10) Currently on the bench

Supplies: Cardstock (Bazzill); patterned paper (My Mind's Eye); stickers (7gypsies, Scrapworks); embellishment (Magic Mesh); Misc: Palatino Linotype and Times New Roman fonts

Art created by Sharyn Tormanen

On collection pages, you will be scrapping photo groupings. An initial decision to make is whether to break one photo out from the pack and emphasize it as a focal point over the others (check out suggestions for this on page 85). Once you've figured that out, it's time to organize the rest. Here are some ways to determine which photos are related to each other logically.

* **Location** Group related photos together in a distinct row, column or block on the page.

* **Matting** Place related photos onto a shared mat. Another alternative is to draw or print a frame around the group.

* **Size** Crop to common height, width or overall size to unite multiple photos.

a line-up to remember

"This one is for the record," said Sharyn when she created this page after thinking about how quickly her children change. In this rich layout, she included photos and journaling about each child—what they're doing right now, this month, at this time. Cropping all photos to the same size and arranging them in columns for each child goes a long way toward bringing order to this tour de force.

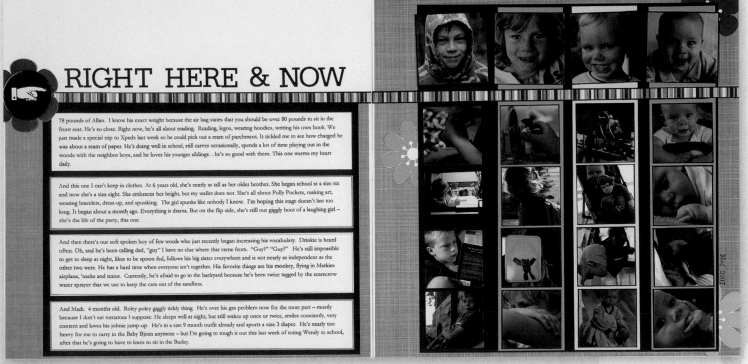

Supplies: Patterned paper (American Crafts, Chatterbox, Sweetwater); letter stickers (American Crafts); chipboard accent (Scenic Route); date stamp (Technique Tuesday); Misc: Garamond font, ink

Art created by Sharyn Tormanen

When you are organizing photos in an ongoing way, you'll be able to see connections between them and get them on the page in a way that really shows the flow of your life.

Art created by Betsy Veldman

family history

Betsy collected five generations of baby photos, starting with one of her great-grandmother and ending with her own daughter. Capturing a century's female lineage on one page makes a great family heirloom.

Supplies: Cardstock (Bazzill, Die Cuts With A View); patterned paper (KI Memories, SEI); die-cut letters (Provo Craft); chipboard (Heidi Swapp); buttons (Die Cuts With A View); metal labels (Junkitz, K&Co.); pin (EK Success); tag (SEI); brad (Karen Foster)

i'll take one of each

What do you do with those one or two photos taken at different times that don't warrant a page of their own? Collect them by theme and get an overview of a season or activity. Betsy's family spent a lot of time at various pools during the summer of '06. She scrapped the highlights of each pool, along with a sportscast journaling tone, to get this rich overview of one hot summer.

Supplies: Cardstock (Stampin' Up); die-cut accents, felt, patterned paper (Tinkering Ink); letter stickers (Making Memories); number stickers (BasicGrey); Misc: Arial font

Art created by Betsy Veldman

for the BIRDS

PURPLE FINCH
(Carpodacus purpureus purpureus)
Length, 6¼ inches
The purple finch is a beautiful song

Now that there are no cows on
the farm, Mom + Dad have
become passionate about their
birds. Feeders and houses are
tucked everywhere summer '06

PURPLE FINCH

strength in numbers

When you really want to make your point, do it with repetition. A layout featuring a photo of one feeder with a cardinal or maybe a shot of my parents filling the feeders tells a certain story. This layout, though, with five feeders and houses tells another story—that of my parents' bordering-on-over-the-top commitment to their birds ever since my Dad retired from farming.

Supplies: Cardstock (Prism); patterned paper (BasicGrey); letter stickers (KI Memories, Scenic Route); glitter flowers (Li'l Davis); flower clip (K&Co.); Misc: 1942 Report and Well Behaved fonts, acrylic paint, brads, ink

only in hindsight

You never know something's a trend until it's happened. This layout is a testament to getting and keeping your prints, negatives and photo files in order. When my son appeared this year in a dandelion crown—five years after making his first one—I knew I wanted to scrapbook a series. In our neck of the woods, dandelions come up in May, and so I checked out my May photos for the last five years and came up with this selection from three of those five years.

Supplies: Cardstock (Bazzill); patterned paper (A2Z); die-cut letters and shapes (Provo Craft); chipboard letters (Heidi Swapp); Misc: Desyrel font

your SPRING flowers

Joshua, when you were 5 years old, our neighbor Shelby taught you how to string dandelions. You worked patiently that day and then presented yourself smiling and proud. Since then, each year when the dandelions come up you make chains -- necklaces and crowns, bracelets and rings. And each time you present yourself, I am newly surprised 1) because I didn't pay enough note to the flowers' appearance; and 2) because your pleasure in this craft never flags. L-R 2005, 2001, 2006.

a formula that works

I love scrapbook pages that gather an entire year's worth of portraits of my children. Even at ten years old, my oldest son changes dramatically in the span of a few short months. Each of these annual pages features five photographs accompanied by one stunning enlargement. What's more, I used the same design for both pages, which made the creation easy and quick.

Supplies: Cardstock (Prism); chipboard numbers, patterned paper (Crate Paper); letter sticker (Scrapworks); photo turn (7gypsies); felt circles (Magic Scraps); foil stickers, pin (Heidi Grace); image editing software (Adobe); digital brush by Katie Pertiet (Designer Digitals); Misc: Desyrel and Platthand Demo fonts

Supplies: Cardstock (Prism); patterned paper, ribbon (Fancy Pants); eyelet (We R Memory Keepers); chipboard accents (Li'l Davis, Prima); button (Autumn Leaves); digital ledger brush by Katie Pertiet (Designer Digitals); ledger grid brush by Anna Aspnes (Designer Digitals); Misc: Desyrel and Platthand Demo fonts

monthly newsletter

Put together a "month-in-review" page to get a snapshot of family happenings on one layout—sort of like a monthly newsletter. For easy arrangement, I lined up all the portrait shots and found a common cropping height and then did the same with the landscape shots.

Supplies: Cardstock (Prism); chipboard arrows, patterned paper, plastic squares, rub-on letters (American Crafts); Misc: Century Gothic and Photo Op fonts

the age-old question

"What should I be for Halloween?" My kids start asking in July, and as they consider new costumes, they recall the old. This page collects all of my youngest son's costumes from his six years of trick-or-treating. I enlarged the most recent and cropped the rest to the same height in chronological order.

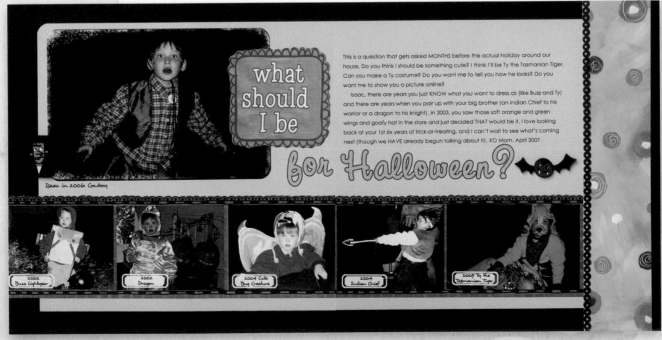

Supplies: Cardstock (Prism); patterned paper, rubber accents (American Traditional); paper frills (Doodlebug); digital borders by Sande Krieger (Two Peas in a Bucket); journal spot by Meredith Fenwich (Scrapbook Graphics); Misc: CAC OneSeventy, CAC Pinnafore, Century Gothic and Desyrel fonts

Chapter 5

Get Moments Scrapped

DATE   SUBJECT/OCCASION   PLACE   COMMENTS

POUT

These are the pages that hold the photos, insights and messages to others that compel you, the ones you come back to again and again.

The key to getting moments scrapped is to *be ready* so that when you feel the impulse, you can *get it scrapped*. As you peruse your collection of photos, look for the stunners that capture raw emotion. This chapter offers a wealth of inspiration on creating moment pages that will tug at your heartstrings and allow you to visually express your deepest sentiments your loved ones will cherish for a lifetime.

Be Ready

1. Flag "stunners" as you go	For digital photos: Use "albums" or "categories" to flag photos in photo organization software. For printed photos: Use a storage system that lets you label and organize prints.
2. Print enlargements regularly	Find a regular time that suits your style and either upload digital photos or drop off negatives to get enlargements. For 12" x 12" (30cm x 30cm) pages, 5" x 7" (13cm x 18cm) is a great photo size that still leaves room for journaling. For greater impact, use 8" x 10" (20cm x 25cm) prints. If you're scrapping smaller pages, 4" x 6" (10cm x 15cm) prints also work well.
3. Record thoughts and messages as you go	Figure out what works for you. Options include a pen and notebook, sticky notes or index cards you can store right with your prints. If you're posting photos on a blog or online album for family and friends, take the time to make some notes with each post. It will make your journaling easier when you make the page.

Get It Scrapped

1. Begin with your message	While it's said that a picture is worth a thousand words, your album viewers are still going to look for journaling. People want to know what it all really means.
2. Match photos with writings you may have already done	When you have must-tell insights, messages and stories that don't "come" with a photo, pair these messages with your stunning photos.
3. Have fun	Enjoy using your favorite supplies, learning new techniques and translating your precious memories into words and images on your pages.

tongue-in-cheek

Bright colors, an oversized photo of Sharyn's daughter touching her tongue to her nose and tongue-in-cheek sports journaling bullets all come together to convey Wendy's fun spirit.

- CONCENTRATION
- Determination
- PRACTICE
- Perseverance
- game face

She's got EXTREME Skills

Personal Best

Supplies: Cardstock (Bazzill); chipboard, stamps (Technique Tuesday); Misc: ink

Art created by Sharyn Tormanen

Understanding Moment Pages

This chapter breaks out three kinds of moment pages with suggestions and examples for each. See which best describes what you want to do to make the most of your photos and the message you want to put on the page.

* Portrait pages: leave a record of just who your subject is in photos and words.

* Relationship pages: when you've got a photo of subjects interacting in a telling way, get it on the page and write down your perception of their relationship at this moment in their lives.

* Message pages: there are things we perceive and think about our loved ones that they would appreciate knowing both now and in the future. This kind of page is the perfect place to record such heartfelt messages.

brother, can you spare a page?

Pair portraits with journaling that goes beyond the obvious (yes, they do look handsome) to create one-photo layouts worth a hundred pages that incorporate several photos. This photo came from a family photo shoot in preparation for holiday cards. While these kinds of portraits often get framed and put on the piano, they don't always make it into the family albums because there's no event to tie them to and they take up a good chunk of "real estate." This one was worth the expense.

Supplies: Cardstock (Bazzill); patterned paper (KI Memories, We R Memory Keepers); chipboard letters and tags (We R Memory Keepers); chipboard circle (Technique Tuesday); letter stickers (Arctic Frog); paper frills (Doodlebug); ribbon (Prima); metal accents (BasicGrey, Imaginisce); Misc: Century Gothic font, pen

A Touch Of LOVE

Drew has always adored his Dad. And it's not just that his Michael will throw a ball with him for hours or help him build a winning car for the pinewood derby or make big old potato-shooting gun just for the fun of it. It's a similarity and a connection between the two of them, it's that Michael is there every day doing what a Dad does, and Drew is there loving him for that. photo 2005. journaling 2006.

EVERYDAY

hero
Nostalgia

Moment pages usually showcase one or two compelling photos.
Good quality photos are great but not required to get a message across. If you add supporting photos, be sure they enhance the message and don't just duplicate the focal photo. Computer cropping will help you zoom in on your subject, but don't remove all context if it contributes to your message.

you know it
when you see it

I found this gem in my folder of holiday photos and was captivated by the sight of these boys looking right at me. Not only did they "look" stunning to me, but I comprehended this as an important moment: the oldest grandchild holding the baby who will probably be the youngest grandchild and looking so proud and relaxed. I added another photo that isn't a "stunner" but that supports and broadens the story of my son's interest in his new cousin.

getting to KNOW YOU

We met Ethan at Christmas--1st boy cousin!!!! Joshua made lots of efforts to connect with him---as he does with all of his cousins. In the bottom photo, he was holding the cabbage patch doll and saying, in a Darth Vader voice, "Ethan, I am not your father." Right before the photo above was taken, Ethan had been fussing in Joshua's arms. Pepper had a bottle of milk she had pumped---just so we could all connect with Ethan--and Joshua got to feed him. They sure do look happy. 12/06.

Supplies: Cardstock (Bazzill); patterned paper (BasicGrey, KI Memories, Me & My Big Ideas); lace, paper pieced owl (EK Success); die-cut letter and shapes (Provo Craft); transparency (My Mind's Eye); pin (Heidi Grace); yarn (Brown Sheep Co.); metal square (Pressed Petals); Misc: chipboard, felt

The most important thing about journaling on moment pages is:

tell more than what is observable from the photo. If your subject looks adorable in a red sweater in the photo, you don't need to say that. Think, instead, about your subject and how you regarded him or her in that moment. What are the telling characteristics, quirks and habits that cannot be seen in the photo? Is there a story or quote from the time the photo was taken that you want to preserve? In other words: "Stick to the feelings, ma'am. Just the feelings."

sit right down and write yourself a letter

Words on the page lead to different discoveries than those in your mind. When I saw these photos of my mom and dad, I was struck by how they were looking at me, but I couldn't say exactly what I was feeling. Beginning with "Dear Mom & Dad," I wrote my journaling in a letter format that yielded an unexpected message for them and for myself.

Supplies: Cardstock (Bazzill); patterned paper (Creative Imaginations, Die Cuts With A View); chipboard letters (Heidi Swapp, Pressed Petals); chipboard accents (Fancy Pants, Pressed Petals, Technique Tuesday); die-cut flower (QuicKutz); rub-on letters (My Mind's Eye); stamps (Technique Tuesday); metallic floss (DMC); Misc: ITC Franklin Gothic font, beads, button, flower, ink, lace, pen, tag

Let your focal photo shine alongside your title, journaling, embellishments and other photos.

Use the following to oomph your photo's shine factor:

* **Size:** Depending on your page size, enlarge a focal photo so that it occupies its space well. You're looking for a balance in which the photo is big enough not to be dwarfed by the page, yet not so big that it overwhelms and crowds the other elements.

* **Position:** Use the rule of thirds. Imagine lines dividing the page into thirds horizontally and vertically. Position your focal point photo at one of the intersections of these imagined lines and it will be sitting in a "sweet spot."

* **Matting:** Put the photo on a larger piece of cardstock to create a mat. You can double or triple mat a photo. Mat color will also contribute to how the photo is viewed on the page.

look here

The photo on this layout shines for many reasons beyond the obvious exuberance of my friend Elaine. It's positioned using the rule of thirds and it contrasts nicely with its background. In addition, a vibrant frame of colorful circles and swirls in two corners, and the title running beneath draw the eye to this photo.

she makes a JOYFUL noise

Where there is Elaine, there is laughter and play. Here she is after untangling party favors the kids were anxiously awaiting. Her victorious appearance had everyone cheering. 06·06

Supplies: Image editing software (Adobe); letters by Rhonna Farrer (Two Peas in a Bucket); papers by Jeannie Papai (Polka Dot Potato); photo actions (Mindy Bush); inking (Atomic Cupcake); circle template by Amy Wolff (Lilypad); Misc: Bohemian font

A successful portrait page conveys more than how your subject looks.

Use your journaling to elaborate on who your subject is. Color and the type of designs and embellishments on the page will also contribute to the page's mood, and thus the viewer's perception of your subject when they see it.

Supplies: Cardstock (Bazzill); felt, patterned paper (Imagination Project, Tinkering Ink); chipboard (Heidi Swapp); Misc: staples

mug shot

One photo accompanied by journaling that includes: name, age, date and brief commentary on your subject's personality add up to one vivid, in-the-moment portrait.

Art created by Kim Kesti

off-topic

These photos are from an outing to Boston College to show Joshua's older cousin around the campus. That story is for another page—an event page. The story here is of how Joshua loves posing with certain kinds of statues. These photos demanded I tell the story of this reoccuring impulse on his part.

Supplies: Cardstock (Bazzill, Prism); patterned paper (7gypsies, My Mind's Eye); transparency (My Mind's Eye); die-cut letters (Provo Craft, QuicKutz); sticker (7gypsies); Misc: chipboard

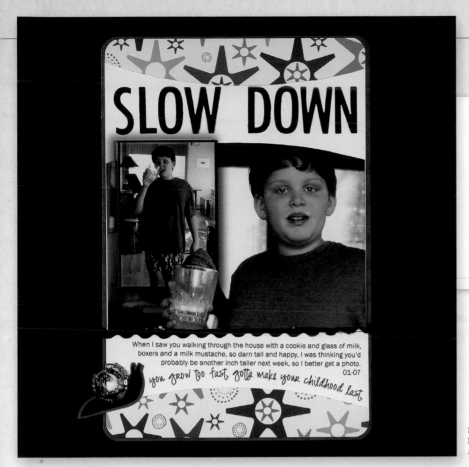

I didn't just happen to take this photo. Rather, when I saw my son walking through the house in his boxers with a big old glass of milk and a milk mustache, it hit me that he looked older than he had the day before. I'm grateful the camera was nearby. In the journaling, I told him just what I was thinking, while jokingly saying "Slow Down!" in the title.

Supplies: Cardstock (Bazzill, Prism); patterned paper (Scenic Route); die-cut letters (QuicKutz); Misc: ITC Franklin Gothic and SP Purkage fonts, beads, clip, rickrack

dash facts

Accompany your next family group portrait with a list of the things that are characteristic of your family. My fifth-grade son loves it when his homework allows "dash facts" rather than full sentences and paragraphs. I love it, too, in situations like this where I can convey so much in a limited space and with limited time.

Supplies: Cardstock (Bazzill); patterned paper (My Mind's Eye, Paper Tapestry); chipboard letters (Heidi Swapp); photo turn (BasicGrey); ribbon (Michaels); lace (Trim-Tex); safety pins (Making Memories); die-cut flower (QuicKutz); Misc: SA-Debbie font, brads, paint, sequins

So much of what we appreciate in life comes out of personal relationships. Because relationships constantly evolve as the people in them grow and change, take the time to record just how you're understanding a relationship in the moments you've photographed.

connect the dots

There's nothing like observing my friend's familial relationships to trigger thoughts about my own. While I had no photos of me greeting my son after a multi-day school trip, I did have shots of another mom and son at that reunion. Using these photos as a springboard for my journaling, I now have a page that leaves a record of how I was feeling about my son's return that day.

Supplies: Cardstock (Bazzill); patterned paper (Fancy Pants, Paper Co., Provo Craft, Scenic Route); negative strip (Creative Imaginations); metal letters (Jo-Ann); chipboard letter (Li'l Davis); flowers (Deluxe Designs); metallic floss (DMC); stamps (Hero Arts, Staples, Technique Tuesday); die-cut flower (QuicKutz); Misc: ITC Benguiat font, acrylic paint, buttons, decorative scissors, eyelet, ink, lace

hayseeds

While Joshua is less & less interested in what the younger cousins are doing–there are still plenty of lovely moments like this: him and Hannah chewing on pieces of hay.

play!

Grab a photo you love and take some time to create for fun! Because moments layouts often use minimal photos, there's lots of room on the canvas to play with design and supplies. The challenge I set for myself here was to work with neutrals and texture. Muted patterns, textured paper, stitching, envelopes and tags provide a subtly detailed background for the black-and-white photo of two cousins.

Supplies: Cardstock (Bazzill, Prism); patterned paper (7gypsies, A2Z, Crate Paper, My Mind's Eye); chipboard letters (Heidi Swapp); buttons (Autumn Leaves, other); lace (Trim-Tex); metallic floss (DMC); flower brads (Nunn Design); pin (Heidi Grace); journaling tag (Li'l Davis); Rx tag (7gypsies); Misc: ITC Benguiat font, acrylic paint, envelope, heart clip, photo corner, tag, thread

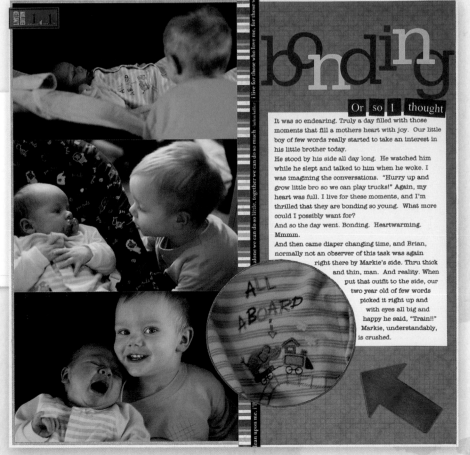

bonding
Or so I thought

It was so endearing. Truly a day filled with those moments that fill a mothers heart with joy. Our little boy of few words really started to take an interest in his little brother today.

He stood by his side all day long. He watched him while he slept and talked to him when he woke. I was imagining the conversations. "Hurry up and grow little bro so we can play trucks!" Again, my heart was full. I live for these moments, and I'm thrilled that they are bonding so young. What more could I possibly want for?

And so the day went. Bonding. Heartwarming. Mmmm.

And then came diaper changing time, and Brian, normally not an observer of this task was again right there by Markie's side. Thru thick and thin, man. And reality. When put that outfit to the side, our two year old of few words picked it right up and with eyes all big and happy he said, "Train!!" Markie, understandably, is crushed.

were we always friends?

Certainly these two brothers will come to understand more about their relationship as they get older. These earliest interactions, though, are lost to them unless those around them remember and tell. A layout that pairs photos and story is the perfect memory aid.

Supplies: Patterned paper (Fontwerks, Polar Bear Press); letter stickers (American Crafts); sticker accents (7gypsies); arrow (Technique Tuesday); Misc: Amertype MdBT and Times New Roman fonts, ink

Art created by Sharyn Tormanen

Even if you think you've already told your subject something, go ahead and get it on the page. They'll hear your voice shine through in a new and different way when it's thought out, written down, and there to be reconsidered on future days.

everyday allegory

What's in the hands of your subject? In this unplanned portrait, my son is holding items that are more than just a book and a stuffed tiger. They are emblems of where he has been and where he is going. Creating this page gave me a new appreciation for the allegorical portraits I studied in art history class.

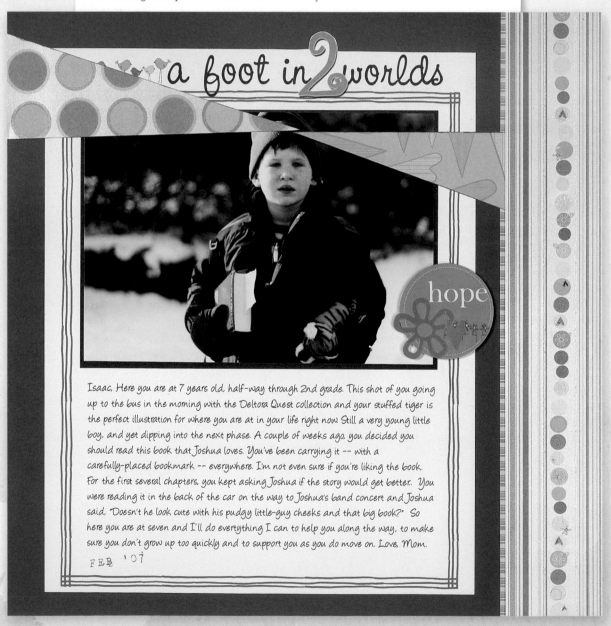

Supplies: Cardstock (Prism); patterned paper, rub-ons, stickers (Heidi Grace); image editing software (Adobe); digital frame by Sande Krieger (Two Peas in a Bucket); Misc: CAC Pinnafore and Doodlebets fonts

place matters

Look to your subjects' surroundings for journaling inspiration. Unless the photo is a studio shot, place is an aspect of it. When my nieces pulled out their bright lounge chairs next to a hayfield, it took me back to my childhood on this very land. I wrote to them about what it is to have a hayfield next to your house as a child as well as what this land may mean to them in the future and the effect their choices will have on that. The result is a page that links the three of us via the place from which we all come.

Supplies: Cardstock (Bazzill); die-cut letters (Provo Craft); die-cut flourish (QuicKutz); Misc: Roman Serif font

Land's Legacy

Dear Sara & Hannah, Here you are sunbathing in your back yard, which is next to a hay field in upstate New York. I sunbathed next to these fields as a girl. But I never really tanned, and, as I got older, I learned that almost half of the year, these skies are overcast. I learned other things, too, and then I decided to leave this farm and go in search of fortune, adventure, and love in a city far away—as one or both of you may one day do.

Now I live in rural New Hampshire, with Uncle Neil, & Josh & Isaac. Our artunes are modest, and I mostly avoid adventure. My current life not all that unlike the one I lived on the farm that I left. *What you know first—that is: the land that you know first—shapes your character.* So seek it in now, and if you do not grow up to live here, I wish you the same fortune as mine: to be able to visit nieces who are living some part of your own past. With much love, Aunt Debbie

he COLLECTS

Today it's lichen, pine cones, a rusted marker from the nature conservancy, sticks. Joshua, your room is full of collections: rocks, pencil leads, knights, airplanes of paper and metal, clay creations, die cast trucks, keychains, old jcostume jewelry. The list goes on and your room grows ever more full.

03 06 Hike in Doe Farm

double duty

When you've got photos of someone acting in a very specific way that is representative of his or her broader personality, make sure your layout does "double duty." In "He Collects," the photos show my son gathering items on a spring hike, but the journaling takes the story farther. It tells the story of a sentimental, collecting, curious boy whose room is full of what he's collected so far in his ten years of life. Next time you snap a revealing incident, use it as a springboard to creating an enduring character portrait.

Supplies: Image editing software (Adobe); labels, letters, notepaper, patterned paper, photo turns, staples, and swirl by Kim Christensen (Scrapbook Bytes); Misc: Mistral and Times New Roman fonts

How Betsy Veldman Gets Moments & Portraits Scrapped

it's all about the message

Betsy admits that there are times she scraps a page inspired by a great photo, a desire to try a new technique or just use some pretty paper, but most times, there is a message or thought she wants to share.

Her pages usually start with a title and journaling and send her looking for the right photo. The "right" photo for Betsy may not be what we typically expect. To accompany journaling about her son starting school, she's more likely to choose a metaphorically powerful photo of him looking out into a big field than one of him getting on the bus.

Betsy takes lots of stunning portraits, enlarges them, and keeps them on hand for just the right message. Check out what she did in "Numbers" on the next page.

Betsy's designs all include a lot of play with product and technique, using bold colors, oversized elements and computer tricks. Check out "Building Character" on page 95 and "Under the Sea" on page 39 to see how she plays with type and digital elements. All this results in pages that reach out and grab you so that you can come on in and get the message.

Numbers You started with a fascination for letters and now you've mastered that and are reading anything and everything you can get your hands on. Now you've moved on to a new fascination - numbers. You and Daddy do math problems every night at bed time and you are catching on so quickly! You started out with simple addition and have moved on to adding bigger and bigger numbers and even doing subtraction. A few days ago you started asking about multiplication, so we worked on that and in no time at all you caught on to multiplying any number x's ten. So what's next buddy? Keep on learnin'!

Art created by Betsy Veldman

Supplies: Cardstock (Stampin' Up); patterned paper (7gypsies, My Mind's Eye); chipboard numbers (Pressed Petals); die-cut strips (Die Cuts With A View); snaps (Making Memories); Misc: EuroRoman font

life's unphotographed moments

Betsy didn't have a photo of her son doing math, but she did have this sweet portrait. Use portrait-style photos when you're documenting an achievement and don't have a photo specific to the subject. By keeping a supply of these photos available, Betsy is steadily scrapping her children's changing faces as well as telling them about their daily successes as they happen—before anything can be taken for granted.

it'll go in her permanent record

When you've got the goods in the photo, take the time to put them on the page with journaling that won't let anyone deny childhood quirks later on. Betsy makes beautiful work of this classic childhood face with colors that evoke both moodiness and beauty.

Supplies: Cardstock (Bazzill, Stampin' Up); patterned paper, rub-ons (Cross My Heart); letter stickers (Scenic Route); stamps (Li'l Davis, Paper Salon); chipboard (Deluxe Designs); buttons (Die Cuts With A View)

Art created by Betsy Veldman

yin & yang

Strong colors and bold graphic designs are a great complement to pages about men and boys. For journaling, Betsy paired a series of words that convey the essence of the relationship she's observed between her husband and her son: a pairing that's echoed in their joined hands.

The Guys

Best Buds

The Dudes

Parent, Child

Teacher, Student

Leader, Follower

Daddy, Little Boy

Provider, Receiver

Protector, Protected

Father, Son

Supplies: Cardstock (Bazzill); felt accents, patterned paper (Tinkering Ink)

Art created by Betsy Veldman

Common Interest

Grandma's been waiting for you...a little granddaughter to keep her company in the midst of all the grandsons. But, who knew you'd fall head over heals for Grandpa? As if he didn't have enough company with all the boys! But...that was before you learned about all the cool things Grandma knows.. Like playing the piano. You didn't realize she had this little talent and a whole book of Sunday School songs to go along with it. You are totally in love with music right now and you love to sit on the piano bench with her, listening to her play. Sometimes you even quietly and timidly sing along. You two have found a common interest and I think Grandma is winning you over.

what do you want to do?

Take a photo of your subjects in a shared activity to convey what's going on in their relationship. Title, photo and journaling all add to the details about this common activity that is bonding Betsy's daughter to her grandmother.

Supplies: Patterned paper (BasicGrey, Fancy Pants, Flair Designs); rub-on letters (Die Cuts With A View, My Mind's Eye); die-cut shapes (Daisy D's, Fancy Pants); letter stickers (American Crafts); stamps (Purple Onion); rhinestones (Imaginisce); Misc: Harrington font

Art created by Betsy Veldman

i think
that one's me

Group portraits of family members who are scattered in different cities and get together only on occasion deserve the kind of treatment Betsy gave this one. The enlargement is really wonderful and even better is her numbering and naming of every cousin in that pickup bed.

1. Abby
2. Amanda
3. A.J.
4. Brooke
5. Paxton
6. Andrea
7. Amber
8. Jonathan
9. Hunter
10. Kestra

cousins

Supplies: Cardstock (Bazzill); patterned paper (Tinkering Ink); heart brad (Creative Impressions); flowers (American Crafts); stamps (Paper Studio); rub-ons (My Mind's Eye); chipboard label (Making Memories)

Art created by Betsy Veldman

building Character
Lessons learned from Legos

⬟ Patience

You've learned to have patience when it comes to getting the new lego sets on your list. They're reserved for special gifts like Christmas and birthdays, but that doesn't prevent you from sleeping with the Lego catalog under your pillow!

⬟ Forgiveness

It's tough to see the masterpiece that took you hours to create being destroyed in less than a minute by your whirlwind sister, but you forgive and move on and rebuild.

⬟ Perseverance

It takes a LOT of time to dig through those thousands of pieces to find just the right one, but you do it all the time!

⬟ Creativity

I am constantly amazed at the ingenious things you put together....club-houses, spaceships, trucks, you name it, you can build it!

oh! the things
you do

Very often the most loved activities of your subject can be the most telling about their personality. See if you can discover connections between action and character as Betsy did here.

Supplies: Cardstock (Bazzill); patterned paper (BasicGrey); brads (Die Cuts With A View); die-cut stars (Sizzix); digital elements by Katie Pertiet (Designer Digitals); Misc: Garamond and Gigi fonts

Art created by Betsy Veldman

Chapter 6

Get Yourself Scrapped

Scrapbooking is my passion, my hobby, my most favorite products, finding the days. But sometimes I get caught up in the latest products, finding the perfect accent, capturing that perfect photo. But then moments like this remind me of why I do what I do. The joy you get from looking at your albums outweighs all else. You pour over these books and examine all the little details, but not in the same way I do. You don't critique the page based on the choice of patterned paper or whether or not the photo is in perfect focus. You just see the memories.

And that's why I do what I do.

Yes. You really should get yourself scrapped.

It's time to come out from behind the camera and chronicle the unknown factoids and tidbits of your character as well as your deepest feelings, daily habits, greatest achievements and overall outlook on life. Let scrapbooks be your tool for sharing who you are and the portrait of your life. There's no better time than right now to start documenting everything that composes your unique personality because some of this stuff is going to change, and this opportunity to reflect on yourself just as you are now won't come again. Turn the page for some eye-opening examples that will get you thinking about recording yourself in your scrapbooks.

If you're thinking there's not a lot to scrap about yourself, take a look at this table and start thinking about yourself over time (past, present, imagined future) and then hold up the diamond that is you and turn it to look at all your facets, ranging from basic facts to personal beliefs.

	YOU OVER TIME	
	past	present
physical: appearance, health, clothing and hairstyles		
personality: likes, dislikes, habits, interests		
perceptions: beliefs, feelings, outlook on life		
experiences: stories, special moments, accomplishments		
people: friends, family, influences		
places: home, school, work, favorite retreat or excursion, regular stop		
things: talismans, tools, decorations		

FACETS OF YOU

So now some of you may have gone from saying: "What is there to scrap about me?" to "How will I ever get all that scrapped?" You don't have to get all of it scrapped. And you don't have to get it done in any kind of order. The thing is to be open to all the aspects of you that could be put onto the page and to gather the bits that will let you make those pages.

tagline

Scrap a phrase, gesture or even attitude that friends and family have come to associate with you. This can be the kind of thing you don't even realize until you stop and think about it—or maybe even until a friend points it out. Figure out your tagline and write about its origins and what you mean by it as Sharyn did in "Be Good," a layout titled with her personal tagline.

I'm not sure when I started saYing it, it's been Years LOTS of Years. Most often it is said as someone is Leaving our home~as in 'BYE ~ Be good' reminder But not preachY. Thats saY it to everYone I sign it to put it at tom of my blings and these days paint ve my door a parting, gentle, preachY Never not mY stYle I regardless of age e-mails I the bot- blog ram one of I plan to it abo front its me

2006

Be Good!

Supplies: Cardstock; stamps (Technique Tuesday); Misc: chipboard, ink

Art created by Sharyn Tormanen

about dinner

When we bought this house, Neil & I saw the river. Friends saw the kitchen and clucked over how small it was. The kitchen? Little did I realize how much time I would need to spend in it. Since then, Neil has done work that has made it better. And it's good enough. Because I'm not a real great cook, and I don't really like cooking, and everyone in the family has different needs (especially Neil) and so Neil does a lot of the cooking and I do what I can and now Joshua's starting to cook. And what I hold onto is that we eat almost every dinner together in our little kitchen. Photos 4*07. Journaling 7*07.

scrap a weakness

My son took these photos of me cleaning the kitchen after dinner. Cleaning is what I do most in the kitchen. The bulk of the cooking this last year, with my husband on sabbatical, was done by him. The meaning in this layout goes deeper than recording logistics, though. It goes to what I feel is one of my failings. I am not a good cook, and I don't like to cook, and, because my children are young, I feel guilty about it. And now it's on the page. Years from now, when they're laughing about what a bad cook I was, at least they'll know that I was a self-aware, bad cook.

Supplies: Image editing software (Adobe); Kraft paper by Christine Smith (Digi Chick); borders and paper by Summer Simmons (Sugar Giggles); photo frames by Katie Pertiet (Designer Digitals); chipboard action (Atomic Cupcake); Misc: DBQ Menu Dingbats, Fontin Sans and Sway fonts

Understanding Yourself Pages

The "germ" or originating idea for a page can arise spontaneously or be the result of meditation and planning. Your approach may range from cut-and-dried details to a thoughtful exploration of something you've discovered about yourself.

* Fact- and/or detail-based pages are a way to get a "snapshot" of yourself at a particular point in time—or even over time. It could be the contents of your purse, a recitation of your daily schedule, or a list of your favorite foods, things, people and activities.

* Personal statement pages tell what you think and feel about a particular subject. I wrote about entertaining in "Clarissa Dalloway Moments" on page 107.

* An epiphany page scraps a major realization you've had—an "ah-ha" moment in your life. A great example of this is in Sharyn's "Simple" on page 105.

Scrapbooking is my passion, my hobby, my most favorite way to pass the days. But sometimes I get caught up in the latest products, finding the perfect accent, capturing that perfect photo. But then moments like this remind me of why I do what I do. The joy you get from looking at your albums outweighs all else. You pour over these books and examine all the little details, but not in the same way I do. You don't critque the page based on the choice of patterned paper or whether or not the photo is in perfect focus. You just see the memories.

And that's why I do what I do.

Art created by Betsy Veldman

don't leave them wondering

Got a passion? It's not always obvious to the others in our lives just why we have the passions we do. In her personal statement, here, Betsy lays out just "Why I Do What I Do" and there's no confusion here.

Supplies: Cardstock, brads (Die Cuts With A View); patterned paper (BasicGrey, Bo-Bunny, Crafty Secrets, Scenic Route): chipboard scroll (Fancy Pants); ribbon (Wrights); metal buckle (7gypsies)

Picturing you

Unless you've got a close friend or relative who is a photo bug, it can be a challenge to get photos of yourself. Combat that challenge in one of the following ways:

* hand over the camera and ask—yes, ask!—friends and family to photograph you

* learn how to use the self-timer on your camera

* ask friends who take photos of you on outings to e-mail you a copy or get you a print

* scan old photos

Picturing the emblematic

Sometimes a photo of the person, place or thing that is key to a page about you is the best illustration. If you don't have a photo, you can set one up or find one on the Internet. With just a little surfing, you can find images of almost anything. The quality might not be high, but it can still be the perfect complement to your story. Just remember to keep in mind copyright laws before downloading or printing photographs from the Internet, particularly if you intend to have your page(s) published in print or online.

No picture

Don't let the lack of a photograph of yourself stop you from scrapping what's important. Scrap the message, and present it so it shines on the page.

true colors

The inspiration for this two-page layout came from an Internet quiz called "True Colors." Even though she did not feature a picture of herself, Kim stores this page in an 8" x 8" (20cm x 20cm) "all about me" album. It turns out her colors are green and gold—and this photo of daisies supports the theme perfectly.

When I heard about the "True Colors Test", I was curious to know what color I would be labeled. If I had to guess, I would have said Orange. Not so. I ended up being an almost equal balance of Green and Gold. So, what does that all mean? Here are some characteristics of the Green and Gold personalities; I've chosen the ones that especially resonated with me and put them in my own words.

GREEN: Strengths include a good sense of self-esteem and personal security. Green is an expression of determination and persistence. A green person prefers practical rather than sentimental gifts and will research a big ticket item before purchasing. Green folks prefer witty and clever over sentimental and romantic. They enjoy reading mysteries and solving puzzles. *Hmm...GREEN sounds a lot like me!*

GOLD: Gold represents responsibility, stability and organization. A gold person is a good listener and is very detail oriented. She enjoys working on a team and is very goal oriented. Golds enjoy tradition, and embrace the concepts of home and family with all their strength. A gold person is a very loyal friend and enjoys being a role model and an inspiration to others. *GOLD? That's me, too.*

GOLD & green

Supplies: Cardstock, die-cut shapes (Bazzill); transparency (Hambly); chipboard letters (American Crafts); buttons (Autumn Leaves); Misc: ink, floss, paint

Art created by Kim Kesti

As with many of the page types in this book, there are a variety of approaches you can use, including list journaling, narratives and storytelling. To make the task easier, i.e., to get that introspective pen moving, try the following:

* Record current stories as soon after they happen as possible so that you get down the details that will otherwise fade over time.

* Record the old stories that family and friends tell. Next time your brother is telling that annoying story from your childhood, make some notes soon afterward so that you can include his perspective in your journaling.

* Free associate from any point on the grid on page 98. Write down words, phrases and/or sentences in order to jumpstart your journaling—even to figure out what angle or approach you want to use.

* Keep a regular journal. Reading through entries at a later date will help you see the significance of the things that were going on in your mind and life at that time.

The true story of when I went to Molasses Pond
Photos: 1990; Story: 2007
1st surprise: I pick up my carpooler--soon to be known as "Little Martha"--and we look at the map and find out that Molasses Pond, in Eastbrook, ME, is not just a little north of Portland. It's a LOT north of Portland. Like try---near Bangor!
2nd surprise: We arrive and I find out that Nancy (who've I've recently met in writing class) is my roommate and she tells me that "really the outhouses are not all that bad." Outhouses?
3rd surprise: I make friends--the first since moving to stony New England 2 years earlier. And they're really interesting. And they will turn out to be my friends for 17 years (and counting).
4th surprise: Writing is something people do and become obsessed with and talk about in broad daylight. Writing transforms my life.
thanks: to Big Martha and to Sue and to all MPers who fill my life.

tell me a story

Tell a story as a springboard to bigger meaning. Rather than write a personal statement on this page about the place of these women and writing in my life, I used a more humorous approach and told the story of my trip, including specific details that trigger many memories and capture the flavor of this destination that changed my life.

Supplies: Cardstock (Bazzill); patterned paper (American Traditional, Fancy Pants); die-cut letters (Provo Craft); compass accent (American Traditional); transparencies (My Mind's Eye); Misc: Courier font, chipboard, photo corners

These pages are about you and should be designed to emphasize what's important and present it in a style that supports your theme and meaning.

Page Layout

Be sure to plan for journaling ahead of time so that you can include as much as needed and so that it's easily readable. Think about just what photo or other element on your page most supports your story and emphasize it so that it's your focal point.

Style

The design of these pages should really elaborate on who you are. Use colors, embellishments and styles that you like and that match your subject.

Tone

Choose colors and motifs that contribute to the message and theme of your page. Pondering mortality is going to call for a different look than talking about your childhood Raggedy Ann doll collection.

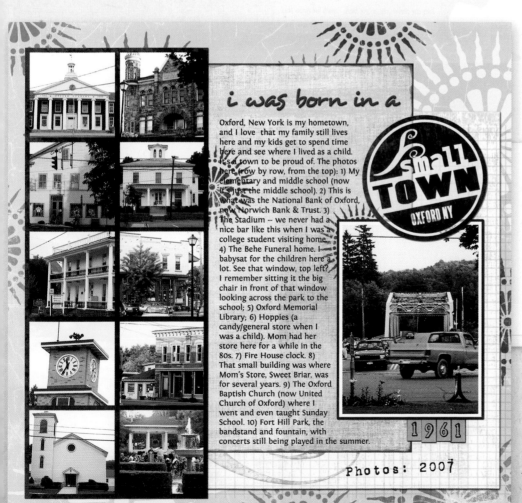

i was born in a

Oxford, New York is my hometown, and I love that my family still lives here and my kids get to spend time here and see where I lived as a child. It's a town to be proud of. The photos here (row by row, from the top): 1) My elementary and middle school (now it's just the middle school). 2) This is what was the National Bank of Oxford, now Norwich Bank & Trust. 3) The Stadium -- we never had a nice bar like this when I was a college student visiting home. 4) The Behe Funeral home. I babysat for the children here a lot. See that window, top left? I remember sitting it the big chair in front of that window looking across the park to the school; 5) Oxford Memorial Library; 6) Hoppies (a candy/general store when I was a child). Mom had her store here for a while in the 80s. 7) Fire House clock. 8) That small building was where Mom's Store, Sweet Briar, was for several years. 9) The Oxford Baptist Church (now United Church of Oxford) where I went and even taught Sunday School. 10) Fort Hill Park, the bandstand and fountain, with concerts still being played in the summer.

small TOWN OXFORD NY

1961

Photos: 2007

the title says it all

The title's message of "I was born in a small town" is the most important part of this page for me. I love including all of the photos, but I'm really making a statement about who I am as a result of where I come from. To that end, I spent time designing the circle part of the title using image-editing software to really emphasize my intent.

Supplies: Image editing software (Adobe); solid papers by Jeannie Papai (Polka Dot Potato) and by Kim Christensen (Little Dreamer); patterned paper by Summer Simmons (Sugar Giggles); flourishes, numbers by Sande Krieger (Two Peas in a Bucket); ink action (Atomic Cupcake); brushes (Toast Snatcher); Misc: 1942 Report, Desyrel, Fontin Sans, PhotoOp and Steelfish fonts

What are the special qualities that make you, you?
Come out from behind the camera and chronicle them on scrapbook pages.

Art created by Kim Kesti

it's a trend

It was when she saw several of her childhood portraits together that Kim realized how many of her clothes her mother had sewn. These photos spanning several years provide a wealth of information including Kim's appearance and the popular styles of clothing and hair during her childhood.

Supplies: Cardstock (Bazzill); patterned paper (Sassafras Lass); chipboard letters (Queen & Co.); brad, flower (Making Memories); pins (Heidi Grace); stamp (Autumn Leaves); ribbon (May Arts); Misc: ink, pen

looking toward the future

This year go farther then sticking your goals up on the fridge. Get a shot of yourself and add photos that represent what you're hoping to accomplish. The result is a scrapbook page that will record just how you're living your life right now.

Supplies: Cardstock, brads (Bazzill); letter stickers (Scenic Route); arrow (Around the Block); journaling block, stars (Heidi Swapp); ribbon (Strano); Misc: staples

Art created by Kim Kesti

at a crossroads

Sharyn and her husband knew exactly what was going on when they made major "simplifying" lifestyle decisions, and this page records their motivations, thoughts and early results. If Sharyn (or anyone else in the family) ever questions the decisions made, all they have to do is look at this record—that is heartfelt and filled with specific details—to feel that they really are living the life that is right for them.

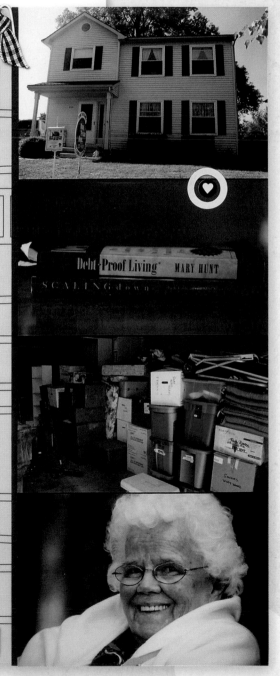

working towards

When I think about it, it's been a series of events and circumstances over the past 6 months that have led us to the same conclusion.

We must simplify. According to the books, to simplify is to be at peace, to live easily…and that is what we've agreed is our number one goal at this time. I truly believe that God has been trying to get this message thru to our thick skulls for some time now. Well…now we've gotten it, and we're working towards a simpler end.

You see…it started back in August of 2004. I woke up one morning, quite literally, and told Greg that I wanted to move. I wanted to put the house for sale and take all of us and all of our clutter to bigger roomier digs. We'd outgrown our home for the stuff we've collected.

month we've been reading. One book, 'Scaling Down' tells us how to purge. It gives lessons on how to tidy the nest, how to live large in a small space. And it's good. The other book, 'Debt-proof living' while it's about finances, still touches on many of the same points. *Keep things simple.* Don't buy what you don't need. I was surprised at how many of the same messages were in both of these books as I had purchased them for 2 separate problems. It turns out that our two problems are more similar than I realized. *Simplify.*

And then came the unexpected check with an apology from my grandma. My grandma was apologizing that there wasn't more money after dividing it amongst 34 of us grandkids. My grandma, who is young, active and God

SIMPLE

And we tried. For one long and weary year, we tried. During that year we filled up my brother's garage, had 29 house showings, signed purchase agreements on two separate homes, and in the end, it wasn't meant. Everything fell thru, and here we are. All of our stuff is still in storage, the sign is leaning up on the side of the house in defeat, and we have one more kid now than when we began our attempt for more space.

And now we're simplifying. Let's fast forward to January of 2006. During this

willing, has many years left with us – gave us an early inheritance so that she could enjoy the giving, and because, well…she doesn't need anything. I thought about that. My grandma lives in a nice cozy simple little apartment, filled with only the basics, and she wants for nothing. She figured it out years ago already.

Keep it simple and make it mean something. Real value is not in things – but in experiences, family, faith and friends.

in 2006

Art created by Sharyn Tormanen

Supplies: Cardstock (Bazzill); accent stickers, vellum (KI Memories); mailbox letters (Making Memories); ribbon (Close to My Heart); Misc: Books Antiqua and Wild Child fonts, paperclip

Supplies: Cardstock (Prism); chipboard circles, patterned paper (Urban Lily); ribbon (Wrights); image editing software (Adobe); digital brushes (Heather Ann Designs); Misc: Fontin, Platthand Demo and You Are Loved fonts

journaling prompts

You want to know about little old me? Well, where do I start? For many of us, talking about ourselves doesn't come easy. These chipboard journaling prompts got this page going quickly, and I ended up sharing things that would not have otherwise occurred to me to include.

evidence photography

In this layout about my need to buy a book whenever I want to do something new, a stack of some of those very books is a more effective statement than a photo of me reading would be. And, what's more, it leaves some clues as to just what I was studying up on.

Supplies: Cardstock, chipboard, patterned paper (Crate Paper); ribbon (Maya Road); image editing software (Adobe); digital paper by Christine Smith (Digi Chick); embellishments by Sande Krieger (Two Peas in a Bucket) and by Christine Smith (Digi Chick); Misc: Angelina, Californian FB and Doodlebats fonts

Once I heard Neil say about me, "She's got to have a book for everything." I don't have to have a book for everything, but I sure do like studying up on my interests. When I'm going into new territory, a book gives me comfort — helps me reduce uncertainty and improve my chances of success. Here's just a sampling of the books I've bought over the years when I've wanted to figure something out about health, children, writing, parties, computers, and poetry. Missing are so many more that I stopped needing: on D.C. and the middle east and divorce and breastfeeding and baby massage business and programming in C. Also missing are those under my bed and in corners, on knitting and scrapbooking and getting published and beading and raising boys. It's true I love my books and my bookstores and my library, and I always will. 04/07

Clarissa Dalloway MOMENTS

I used to get melancholy feelings AFTER giving a big party-the result of exhaustion and of the planning and work that had so occupied my time now being completely done: what next? I called these feelings "my Clarissa Dalloway moments" after the book by Virginia Woolf in which Mrs. Dalloway is neurotically engaged in planning and worrying about and giving a party.

When we gave this past year's holiday party, though, a huge melancholy hit me the day BEFORE the party. I was exhausted and spending so much time on the party instead of just being with my family (and yet my boys LOVE it when we give a party and they weren't complaining.) I was wondering how I would get the energy to enjoy the party and if anyone would enjoy it.

Fast-forward to the middle of the party. Our small house is full of people we really care about and enjoy and these people are eating and talking and having fun and children are running up and down stairs and planning performances and coming up with secret passwords. As I stood in the kitchen with Patty and Susan, I told them how I'd felt before the party, but that now, being with them, it all felt right, that I was happy. Patty immediately said, "Oh, I always feel that way before a party." "Me, too," Susan added. Really? So "Clarissa Dalloway moments" are experienced by others? I find absolute comfort in knowing this. Entertaining is stressful and fun and maybe frivolous, but the Clarissa Dalloway in me is always going to need to do it.

self-exploration just for me

I'm not sure any of my family are going to really care about this story other than as a curiosity in the years to come. I, however, needed to write this down, to get at all the emotions that I have around entertaining and to record an incident from one party that comforts me every time I'm embarking on a new one.

Supplies: Cardstock (Bazzill); chipboard, patterned paper, ribbon (Fancy Pants); image editing software (Adobe); digital border by Sande Krieger (Two Peas in a Bucket); Misc: Copperplate Gothic and Sweetheart Script fonts, rhinestones

make a list

Stuck for what to say about yourself? Start with a list and write down what you know right off. After a couple items, you'll find yourself jumpstarted and writing down things you may not have even consciously thought about lately. Betsy listed all the things her hands do and ended up with a picture of all she does in her life right now as a mom and scrapbooker.

cook 90% of the meals for my family
use the phone to call for take-out for the other 10% of those meals
hate to clean the bathroom
love to flip through magazines
push the snooze button way to many times in the morning
love to sew
sport my wedding ring which NEVER comes off
always look like they need a manicure
put band-aids on ouchies
scrap precious family memories
make three beds every morning
get to hold precious little hands
capture my family history in pictures
are usually full of paint or ink
make flower arrangements for any occassion
wash two messy kiddos several times a day
assist in drinking my dt. cherry coke
fold at least 7 loads of laundry every week
spend way too much time typing on the keyboard :)

THESE hANds...

Supplies: Patterned paper (Die Cuts With A View, KI Memories); letter stickers (Die Cuts With A View, Doodlebug, K&Co.); rub-ons (Creative Imaginations); Misc: ink

Art created by Betsy Veldman

Chapter 7
Get Your World Scrapped

What did your childhood home look like?

What about the town you grew up in? Do you have a household appliance that changed your life or a precious family heirloom that has been passed down through the generations? Is there a stuffed animal your child has loved since infancy? Take everyday life one step farther by leaving a record of the life you lived in the past as well as the life you are living now. This chapter offers easy ways to approach the task of recording your world and documenting its significance for you and your loved ones.

One of the many times Joshua was lamenting that he wanted to go to Grandma and Grandpa's house, I asked him what he so loved there. "Well," he said, "I like being with Grandma and Grandpa, and THE FOOD IS SO GOOD." Not only is the food good, the whole experience is lovely. The table is loaded with more side dishes than we see at home, and there's always dessert and there's always whipped cream. And after we eat, we sit around the table and yak and someone does dishes and the rest of us play. We love how Grandma fills a table. 2002-2007

To make scrapbook pages that leave a record of your life:

1. Consciously think about and gather photos of the places, things and routines that are (or were at some time) ingrained in your daily life.

2. Include journaling that not only records the facts and details about these things, but that tells of their place in your life.

3. Scrap these photos and writings onto pages using products that complement and even deepen your theme, meaning and context.

first impressions

When you're writing about what a place means in your life, remember to record first impressions—especially if they don't quite jibe with your later feelings. When we originally bought our house, this nearby trestle meant "noise" to me. Ten years later, it is an important piece of our landscape, and my journaling tells why and notes this irony.

Neil, we first saw our house with a realtor. It was February and a train went by. We noticed its sound and could see the blur of it across two neighboring yards and through a leafless woods. We were a little concerned—probably me more than you because you loved this house and the river. We moved in in May. Joshua was one year old, and the windows were open. Joshua was nursing and waking up at night and I heard every sound—including every train run. In fact, I would woke seconds before the train in anticipation of it.

Who knew that 10 years later, I would barely notice its sound? That I would remember hikes with one of the boys on my back across these tracks and down the steep hill into the woods beyond or even over the tracks to the cornfields? This trestle was our way out when the river flooded in 2006. On canoe outings we've seen teens jump from it to the river, and when we ski the river in winter, crossing under the trestle means we're almost home. This trestle is a part of the landscape of our home. *journaling 2007.*

Supplies: Cardstock (Bazzill, Prism); chipboard, patterned paper (Fancy Pants); image editing software (Adobe); digital stitches by Tia Bennett (Two Peas in a Bucket); frames by Katie Pertiet (Designer Digitals); Misc: CBX Heber, Century Gothic and Pharmacy fonts

Possible subjects

1. **Routines:** by time (daily, weekly, monthly, annually) or by type (work, school, family, activities)

2. **Things:** items in your home, garage, personal space, work space; items purchased, handmade, inherited or found; practical, essential or frivolous items

3. **Places:** home (inside, outside, neighborhood, community/town), stores, restaurants, work, school, other

what are you reading?

Is there a story, movie or song that has entered the fabric of your family's life? Kim, her husband and their seven children have read all the books in the Harry Potter series, and the saga of Harry is something that compels every one of them. What better way to show how the story has woven its way into their lives than to record the Kesti family's predictions for the final book?

HP7

OUR FAMILY PREDICTIONS

RECORDED ON 07-07-07

HARRY POTTER BOOK SEVEN PREDICTIONS

KEITH: AUNT PETUNIA WILL PLAY A CRITICAL ROLE IN BOOK SEVEN. SHE'LL HELP HARRY BASED ON THEIR BLOOD CONNECTION BY FINALLY USING MAGIC.

KIM: SNAPE WILL SHOW HE'S TRULY GOOD IN THE END BY SACRIFICING HIMSELF TO HELP HARRY KILL VOLDEMORT. ALSO, HARRY AND GINNY WILL GET BACK TOGETHER.

TRISTAM: HERMOINE WILL GET KILLED PROTECTING RON. SNAPE IS A GOOD GUY AND WILL SAVE HARRY FROM GETTING KILLED BY VOLDEMORT. SIRIUS BLACK WILL SOMEHOW COME BACK AND GIVE ADVICE TO HARRY (BUT HE WON'T RETURN TO LIFE). DRACO MALFOY WILL HAVE A CHANGE OF HEART AND BECOME A GOOD GUY IN THE END, TOO.

CHRIS: HARRY AND VOLDEMORT WILL BOTH GET KILLED OFF DESPITE THE FACT THAT SNAPE WILL SHOW HIS TRUE COLORS AND TRY TO SAVE HARRY. MOST LIKELY RON AND HERMOINE WILL GET TOGETHER.

MEGHAN: HARRY, VOLDEMORT AND SNAPE WILL ALL BE KILLED IN A BATTLE. HERMOINE WILL SURVIVE AND END UP MARRYING ONE OF THE TWINS.

ETHAN: HARRY WILL TRY TO KILL VOLDEMORT BUT WON'T BE ABLE TO SINCE PETTIGREW WILL HEAL VOLDEMORT. SNAPE WILL END UP KILLING VOLDEMORT AND WILL TRY TO KILL HARRY, TOO.

CLARA: SNAPE IS A BAD GUY AND HE WILL RUN AWAY AND NEVER BE SEEN AGAIN. HARRY WILL KILL VOLDEMORT AND EVERYONE WILL BE HAPPY.

Supplies: Cardstock (Bazzill); patterned paper (Tinkering Ink); chipboard letters (Rusty Pickle); Misc: Delicious font, brads

Art created by Kim Kesti

Leaving a record of the places, items and routines in your life that compel you, for both good and bad, can be a huge undertaking. Focus the message on your page by thinking about the following:

* Why is this important?

* How did this become important? Was it happenstance, habit, heritage or something else?

* Is this a positive, negative or relatively neutral part of your world?

unplanned tradition

It was not in any way planned that Neil would be the one to present the kids' birthday cakes at their parties. It just started happening. When the kids were little, they were on my lap, and so he did the cake carrying. As they got older, I was busy orchestrating games while he took care of food. It's only recently, though, that I realized this was our tradition, one that evolved through happenstance, and one that I wouldn't change for the world.

Supplies: Cardstock (Prism); patterned paper, rhinestone swirls (Prima); image editing software (Adobe); digital chipboard, stencil and tear actions (Atomic Cupcake); Kraft paper by Christine Smith (Digi Chick); doodle circle by Andrea Victoria (Designer Digitals); flower, paper and ribbon by Tia Bennett (Two Peas in a Bucket); frame, party papers, photo edge and tag by Katie Periet (Designer Digitals); digital brush by Anna Aspnes (Designer Digitals); Misc: Berlin Sans, Fontin Sans and French Script MT fonts

Got photos?

* Yes.

If you've got photos to choose from, think about how many you really need to tell the story. A well-loved stuffed animal that has traveled the globe would be nicely shown with multiple photos of it in different locales. An ode to the claw-footed tub, however, probably only requires one shot.

* No, but I could take some.

In this situation, think about context, season, time of day and anything else in your subject's environment that might provide a more complete record or deepen the reader's appreciation for this subject in your life.

* Nope, and I can't take any.

If you don't have photos or even access to the subject, you could scan older photos or perhaps even find a photo on the Internet. I actually found a photo of the exact transistor radio I got from my tenth Christmas at a collector's Web site. As mentioned earlier, keep in mind copyright law as it applies to photography found on the Internet or photos taken by a professional studio.

regular hang-out

If it's a favorite spot, then you probably have photos from different seasons and over many years. Take the time to include this kind of variety of photos. In "Meet Me on the Porch," I've scrapped photos from several different gatherings to remind me of how it has been when my family comes together on this porch.

Supplies: Cardstock (Prism); patterned paper (Prima, We R Memory Keepers); die-cut letters (Provo Craft); image editing software (Adobe); digital brushes by Sande Krieger (Two Peas in a Bucket); Misc: Alba Super, Alfredo's Dance, Automobile, Fifth Ave., Halda Smashed, Loungy and Weathered Fence fonts, brads

mEeT Me on the porch

We spend a lot of time on Grandma & Grandpa's front porch when we are in Oxford. And it's not just because it's beautiful -- the company here rocks! Love this porch! (like a rabbit loves to run).

Pages that document your world are usually grounded in the concrete world of place, routine and things.

While you may also comprehend a beauty, harshness or grace in the thing you are scrapbooking, avoid using these abstract words and begin instead with the real and particular details such as the chipping paint on the barn or the aroma of your kitchen. Write about these particulars and they will trigger memories and feelings. Get those onto the page, too, and you'll discover that those abstracts like "beauty" will come through in your words, and, what's more, you'll have a rich and detailed record of an aspect of your world.

what he said

Use a bit of remembered conversation as your initial, grounding detail. In this layout below, my son's words are what helped me make the connection to how it feels to be here, at this table, and then to write about it.

One of the many times Joshua was lamenting that he wanted to go to Grandma and Grandpa's house, I asked him what he so loved there. "Well," he said, "I like being with Grandma and Grandpa, and THE FOOD IS SO GOOD." Not only is the food good, the whole experience is lovely. The table is loaded with more side dishes than we see at home, and there's always dessert and there's always whipped cream. And after we eat, we sit around the table and yak and someone does dishes and the rest of us play. We love how Grandma fills a table. 2002-2007

Supplies: Image editing software (Adobe); brad, flower, paper, scallop accent by Leora Sanford (Digitals); letter tabs, paper, photo frames, tag by Katie Pertiet (Designer Digitals); paper by Jeannie Pappai (Polka Dot Potato); bird, frame by Anna Aspnes (Designer Digitals); felt action (Atomic Cupcake); Misc: Beffle and Fontin fonts

These pages can really shine when you've selected a strong focal photo. A focal photo gives the viewer's eye a place to start on the page and also creates a hierarchy indicating which photo is to be viewed first, next and so on.

Keep this criteria in mind when selecting a focal photo for your next layout:

* Is it engaging (like a great shot of one or two people looking into the camera or engaged in a relevant activity)?

* Does it represent or trigger an association with the aspect of your world you are scrapbooking?

* Does it have great photographic quality?

a certain look

Look for papers and embellishments that re-create the essence of a place on the page. The colors and motifs here are all ones I associate with the time when I would have been collecting Avon bottles. The papers echo my room's wallpaper, and the flowers and vines are just the kind of thing I would have loved back then.

I collected AVON

1976/77 MAGIC PUMPKIN COACH DECANTER; bird of paradise cologne - full. This avon decanter is in mint condition, in original box and full. Clear glass coach bottle with gold cap/very detailed glass decanter. Amazing vintage decanter find!!! $10 flat rate fee to anywhere in the United Atates!! Buy it now! $9.99.

When I think about it now, I can't say exactly *why* I collected Avon bottles. Looking at them sitting in my childhood room (thanks, Mom, for dusting them) I can see it wasn't for the cologne since most of them are still full (Sweet Honesty was my preferred scent). I guess I liked how they looked. And I guess I wanted to buy something. Where we lived, the closest (little) mall was an hour away. The Avon lady, though? She came right to our house every two weeks. And we shopped at our kitchen table and I eavesdropped on the grown-up yakking. And-hey!-there's still a market for these. Check out the hundreds of ebay listings. I'm not selling mine, though. At least for as long as my mom continues to keep them on a shelf and dusted. August 2007.

Supplies: Cardstock (Prism); patterned paper (Prima); plastic leaf (American Crafts); rhinestones (Darice); image editing software (Adobe); brushes by Anna Aspnes (Designer Digitals); Misc: Letter Gothic font, flower

Getting *Routines* Scrapped

Call it routine, habit, tradition or repeated happenstance, every family has its own way of doing things at any point in time.

it's an attitude

Why do you do the things you do? Think about it. Burning wood is more than a habit for us—it's an attitude. This layout reminds our whole family of how a roaring fire in our very efficient woodstove is about more than charm for us. It's about keeping warm in a New England house with huge and drafty windows and not going broke in the process.

WE BURN *wood*

Our woodpile in early '06 - right before we really got some cold weather, and it started going down quickly. With all of our big and drafty windows, the woodstove makes a huge difference.

staying warm

home & hearth

Supplies: Cardstock; patterned paper (unknown); image editing software (Adobe); foam action, mixed dings (Atomic Cupcake); flowers, photo corners by Sande Krieger (Two Peas in a Bucket); Misc: Antique Type, Desyrel, Platform Shoes and Rosebud Sweet fonts

How many times have the 3 of us made this drive? Enough times to know how to do it right. Books on tape. Snack food. Drinks. I-90 rest areas. Maybe a little shopping before we hit the NY border. (K-B Toys and Crane Paper Outlet.) If we need it, a meal at the Neptune Diner in Oneonta and then Exit 9 off I-89.

This time, we had to take off in the midst of a 24+hr power outage ... so we packed dirty clothes, made a trip to the library as we started the trip, and then had pizza for breakfast at Ry-Guy's. Good thing they had power.

We shook things up and drove over 101 and down to 495. Joshua still had blue hair from "crazy hair day" and no water at home. We listened to *Artemis Fowl* on the way out and gave it a 10. Too tired to stop for food we plowed on through and got to Oxford before 5! The girls were already at Grandma and Grandpa's, and there was hot lasagna waiting. Once again, it was well worth the drive. NH to NY. 02/06

road trippin'

Every family approaches trips differently. This record of a February road trip from New Hampshire to New York is representative of how it's gone the last several years during the boys' winter break. Our routine will change, though, as the boys get older—and that's why I'm glad I got it down now, because it's a layout that's going to evoke a whole lot of memories in years to come.

what you call it

Are there locations in your landscape that have taken on names outsiders wouldn't understand? That's how it is with the area near the top floor of my parents' barn. We say we're going "up over head," and that phrase made a perfect title for the page. It also acts as a jumping-off spot for my journaling and ensures that this name will endure.

up over head

We've always referred to the barn's top floor and the area around it as "UP OVER HEAD." The door slides to open, and the last plank of the bridge over to it is loose. There's a plank's worth of emptiness that's always made me nervous. I used to go up here to shovel grain into the feed chute. In the summers, Dad & Uncle Donny, Terry, Mark and then Matt logged many hours here. They backed the wagon in by hand, steering with the tongue. Hay was loaded on a conveyor to the steadily-rising floor below. One of my few risky acts of childhood was made here when I jumped from this floor to the one below when there was no hay (playing Batman). Dad heard the fall as he milked cows below and came running up with a friend who was there to buy milk and yak. I was fine, but I do not want my kids jumping like that when they go "up over head." journaled 2007.

What are the things in your life? Did you pick them or did they pick you? Are they necessities or pleasures?

Grandma's China. It's a beautiful, simple pattern, one that will never go out of style. A simple white-on-white pattern with silver etching. Beautiful and timeless. But they are more than just pretty dishes and timeless not only because of the pattern. These dishes hold more than food, they hold years of special memories. Memories of times spent together as a family - special times, times of celebration. Years of Christmas and Thanksgiving dinners spent at Grandma's house with loved ones all around. I can almost smell Grandma's scrumptious turkey and stuffing and hear the laughter of family members. Grandma is gone now, but I am so happy to have this special reminder of her. The china is displayed in my dining room now with the hope that it will see many more happy celebrations and eventually be passed down to my daughter and my daughter's daughter...

Art created by Betsy Veldman

inherit the wind

It's actually more likely you'll inherit the china or a watch than the wind. An inherited item becoming central to your routines and/or traditions is different from a personally selected item playing that role. Since you'll probably be passing this item along to your descendants some day, get the stories down so everyone will know where it came from and the significance it held.

Supplies: Cardstock (Bazzill); border stickers, patterned paper (Die Cuts With A View); letter stickers (BasicGrey); chipboard letters (Making Memories); image editing software (Adobe); digital element by Rhonna Farrer (Two Peas in a Bucket); Misc: vintage buttons

trigger point

When scrapbooking an important object in your world, journal more than the facts. Journal memories and feelings this object triggers and even what it represents in your life. Sure, this is a wind-up alarm clock that sat on my grandmother's dresser. But it's more than that, and the journaling makes this clear, linking it to memories of sleepovers, popcorn and bobby pins. This clock is representative of my grandmother's nature—of her love for order, schedule and precision—and that's the kind of journaling you want to make sure you include.

Grandma Hodge was a person of order and routine: days, weeks, and seasons all had their expectations. When you stayed overnight with Grandma Hodge, you knew what to expect. Jiffy-pop and TV: Brady Bunch & Jackie Gleason. Set the table for the next morning's breakfast. Once into our knighties, she bobby-pinned her hair. And then she wound this clock—which I could hear ticking all night if I slept with her. She'd read a story book and kiss me goodnight and then roll over to read her romance novel. Staying with Grandma meant, "going to bed with the chickens" (i.e., early). Failing to keep a sleepover date with her was "giving her the mitten." While I haven't inherited Grandma Hodge's knack for order, I do have this clock and that's enough to make me appreciate her self-discipline, and push myself to get a little, too.

Supplies: Cardstock (Prism); patterned paper (A2Z); chipboard letters (We R Memory Keepers); plastic letters (Heidi Swapp); rub-ons (Autumn Leaves, Hambly); flower appliqué, suede trim (Hirschberg Schutz); clock pin (EK Success); Misc: ITC Franklin Gothic font, paint

apparatusville

remember when?

What are the things in your home that technology will make outdated in the future? Sharyn loves to catch this kind of progression, hoping that one day her children will see this page of all the baby equipment in their house now and think, "Oh, yeah, that's how baby swings were back then."

I counted. We have just over 20 square feet of baby/toddler apparatus in our home. *In our tiny home.* And the funny thing is, I actually prefer to hold my babies - I'm not all that fond of the whole appliance thing - they grow too quick, and I want to hold them, snuggle them. But I won't argue - it is handy to have something that'll amuse them for a few moments while I cook dinner, something that will hold them while they eat, another to rock them when they don't want to be held...and so on. It all adds up. I always feel such a great sense of space after we put each piece in the basement when the kids outgrow them. And joy, again, when we pull them out for the newest little Torm.

Art created by Sharyn Tormanen

Supplies: Cardstock (Bazzill); chipboard letters (Heidi Swapp); scallop accent (Doodlebug); Misc: Berylium font, paint

why this?

Think about an item you display in your home, whether for a particular holiday, season or just daily, and get its importance onto a page. This is Betsy's favorite Christmas decoration, the one she always puts in an honored spot during the holiday season. It will trigger so many memories for her children in the years to come, and—because of this page— there will be no doubt in their minds as to why this decoration was the one their mom loved most and why it was key to their experience of Christmas.

THE True meaning

This is my favorite Christmas decoration of all time. I received it as a gift from the girls at the store. I love it's simplicity...the way the figures are simple and faceless, but yet so expressive. But more than that I love that it represents the true meaning of Christmas. The true signs of Christmas are becoming harder and harder to find amongst the busyness of the season. Amidst the hustle and bustle of decorating the house, fighting your way through crowded stores in search of the perfect gifts and the perfect way to wrap them, baking a plethora of Christmas goodies and candies, and on and on. The peace that was meant to be the center of the season is almost completely drowned away. This Nativity scene on display next to my tree is a reminder to keep the true meaning of the season... to celebrate the birth of God's Son. As my children grow older it becomes more evident to me that this true meaning needs to be stressed more and more. I want my children to know why we celebrate this season, the real reason we give gifts, and carry on the traditions we do. I want them to be filled with the peace and promises that Christmas holds, not filled with greed and selfishness. There needs to be a balance. Yes, Christmas is a fun and exciting time for children, it was for me as a child, but there needs to be more. More meaning than just ripping off the paper on a pretty package that holds a trinket that will be forgotten almost as quickly as the pretty paper is tossed away. This is my hope for my children as we go through this wonderful season from year to year. That I might impart the true joy and celebration of the season...the birth of God's Son.

Of Christmas

Supplies: Cardstock (Bazzill, Die Cuts With A View); patterned paper (My Mind's Eye); letter stickers (BasicGrey); rub-ons (Die Cuts With A View); charm (Imaginisce)

Art created by Betsy Veldman

Whether it's a favorite spot in your home or a 600-acre farm, photograph it and write about it. Make it permanent on the page and in your memory.

know this

The best kinds of pages you can leave for your family are those that tell what you most want them to know. Sharyn doesn't assume her children understand why they are living in a small house they'd expected to leave several years ago. Instead she made "Our Cozy Home," which evokes a mood of love and comfort while filling her lucky children in on just why they're growing up in this house.

Supplies: Cardstock (Bazzill); patterned paper (7gypsies, Creative Imaginations, Daisy D's, Heidi Grace, My Mind's Eye, Scenic Route, Sweetwater); stamps (Technique Tuesday); button (Doodlebug); flowers (American Crafts, Doodlebug); decorative tape (7gypsies); number stickers (Making Memories); chipboard house (Scrapsupply); Misc: brads, ink, lace, pen

Art created by Sharyn Tormanen

Take time to record the major changes that happen in your community. Rebuilding a church is a bittersweet event for a congregation with memories of baptisms, weddings, funerals and more. With this page, Betsy honors the past and records an important moment in the lives of many in her community. And later on, when she asks her children if they remember the old church, she'll have photos to help jog and cement their memories.

Art created by Betsy Veldman

Supplies: Cardstock (Die Cuts With A View); patterned paper (Die Cuts With A View, Scenic Route); chipboard letters (Scenic Route); chipboard circles (Making Memories); rub-ons (Creative Imaginations); button (Autumn Leaves); ribbon (Offray); Misc: Enviro font

shaped by place

Is there a place that has impacted who you are? Because I feel so strongly about the land I grew up on, I scrapped "What You Know First." I included images that resonate with me. In addition to writing about my own love of this place, I wrote about my hopes for my children: that they will have a strong connection with their childhood land and that they will also take a little bit of my childhood landscape into their hearts.

Supplies: Cardstock (Prism); acrylic flowers (American Crafts); ribbon (May Arts); photo turns (7gypsies); image editing software (Adobe); digital paper and embellishments by Sande Krieger (Two Peas in a Bucket); Misc: Algerian, Antique Typewriter, Automobile, Copperplate Gothic, Desyrel, Designer Mixed Ding, Expert Rounded, Expp and JungleFever fonts, brads, heart clip

It's About the Scrapbooks

Debbie Hodge has been keeping scrapbooks since she got her first camera as a child. She originally scrapbooked to leave a record, to proclaim that she was, indeed, here. In recent years, she's come to crave scrapbooking time, because she finds it immensely satisfying to craft with photos, paper and words. She began publishing scrapbook pages and articles in 2005, and she's now a contributing editor with *Memory Makers* magazine writing the "Take 2" column about two-page layouts. Debbie lives in a small New Hampshire university town with her husband, Neil, and their two sons, Joshua and Isaac.

It's About the Photos

Kim Kesti started scrapbooking and papercrafting in 2003, and since then has become addicted. Addiction or not, Kim also takes care of seven (soon to be eight!) busy children and finds time to hang out and travel with her adorable husband. Because there's no way Kim can spend hours on one layout, she shortens her start-up time by taking cues for color and embellishments straight from the photos she's scrapping. She rarely makes enlargements and frequently fits several photos on a page. See just how Kim gets those multi-photo event pages scrapped in the spotlight on her in Chapter Two.

It's About the Little Things

Sharyn Tormanen started scrapbooking when she got her first camera at nine years old, mounting those shots in an album and taking time to record her thoughts. Sharyn purposely weaves references to current culture, society and technology into the narratives that accompany her photographs. She wants her four children to read them years later and say, "Oh! Yes. That's how it was." When she's not putting photos onto paper pages, Sharyn blogs almost daily, creating an ever-evolving memoir in pictures and words that's irresistible—she's been stopped more than once at the grocery store by people who recognize her from reading "Live From Tormville" online. A look at Sharyn's spotlighted pages in Chapter Three will give you a taste of her unique approach to scrapping the little things.

It's About the Message

Betsy Veldman started scrapbooking and papercrafting six years ago. She's a wife of nearly ten years and a stay-at-home mom to three children under six. Besides taking care of her family, Betsy designs scrapbook pages for magazines and manufacturers. While there are times Betsy's bold pages are inspired by a piece of paper she loves or a new technique she'd like to try, most of the time she starts a page with a message or thought she wants to share and then goes in search of the photos and materials. See how she does this, pairing oversized embellishments and vivid colors with strong portraits and memorable journaling, in the spotlight on Betsy in Chapter Five.

source guide

The following companies manufacture products featured in this book. Please check your local retailers to find these materials, or go to a company's Web site for the latest products available. In addition, we have made every attempt to properly credit the items mentioned in this book. We apologize to any company that we have listed incorrectly, and we would appreciate hearing from you.

7gypsies
(877) 749-7797
www.sevengypsies.com

A2Z Essentials
(419) 663-2869
www.geta2z.com

Adobe Systems Incorporated
(800) 833-6687
www.adobe.com

American Crafts
(801) 226-0747
www.americancrafts.com

American Traditional Designs
(800) 448-6656
www.americantraditional.com

ANW Crestwood
(973) 406-5000
www.anwcrestwood.com

Arctic Frog
(479) 636-3764
www.arcticfrog.com

Around The Block
(801) 593-1946
www.aroundtheblockproducts.com

Atomic Cupcake
www.atomiccupcake.com

Autumn Leaves
(800) 588-6707
www.autumnleaves.com

BasicGrey
(801) 544-1116
www.basicgrey.com

Bazzill Basics Paper
(480) 558-8557
www.bazzillbasics.com

Berwick Offray, LLC
(800) 344-5533
www.offray.com

Brown Sheep Company, Inc.
(800) 826-9136
www.brownsheep.com

Chatterbox, Inc.
(888) 416-6260
www.chatterboxinc.com

Close To My Heart
(888) 655-6552
www.closetomyheart.com

CPE/Consumer Product Enterprises, Inc.
(800) 327-0059
www.cpesource.com

Crate Paper
(801) 798-8996
www.cratepaper.com

Creative Imaginations
(800) 942-6487
www.cigift.com

Creative Impressions Rubber Stamps, Inc.
(719) 596-4860
www.creativeimpressions.com

Cross-My-Heart-Cards, Inc.
(888) 689-8808
www.crossmyheart.com

Dafont
www.dafont.com

Daisy D's Paper Company
(888) 601-8955
www.daisydspaper.com

Darice, Inc.
(800) 321-1494
www.darice.com

Deluxe Designs
(480) 497-9005
www.deluxecuts.com

Designer Digitals
www.designerdigitals.com

Die Cuts With A View
(801) 224-6766
www.diecutswithaview.com

Digi Chick, The
www.thedigichick.com

Digital Paper Tearing
www.digitalpapertearing.com

DMC Corp.
(973) 589-0606
www.dmc-usa.com

Doodlebug Design Inc.
(877) 800-9190
www.doodlebug.ws

Dream Street Papers
(480) 275-9736
www.dreamstreetpapers.com

EK Success, Ltd.
(800) 524-1349
www.eksuccess.com

Fancy Pants Designs, LLC
(801) 779-3212
www.fancypantsdesigns.com

Fiskars, Inc.
(866) 348-5661
www.fiskars.com

Flair Designs
(888) 546-9990
www.flairdesignsinc.com

Fontwerks
(604) 942-3105
www.fontwerks.com

Frances Meyer, Inc.
(413) 584-5446
www.francesmeyer.com

Hambly Studios
(800) 451-3999
www.hamblystudios.com

Heather Ann Designs
www.heateranndesigns.com

Heidi Grace Designs, Inc.
(866) 348-5661
www.heidigrace.com

Heidi Swapp/Advantus Corporation
(904) 482-0092
www.heidiswapp.com

Hero Arts Rubber Stamps, Inc.
(800) 822-4376
www.heroarts.com

Hirschberg Schutz & Co., Inc.
(800) 221-8640

Imagination Project, Inc.
(888) 477-6532
www.imaginationproject.com

Imaginisce
(801) 908-8111
www.imaginisce.com

Jenni Bowlin
www.jennibowlin.com

Jo-Ann Stores
www.joann.com

Junkitz
(732) 792-1108
www.junkitz.com

K&Company
(888) 244-2083
www.kandcompany.com

Karen Foster Design
(801) 451-9779
www.karenfosterdesign.com

KI Memories
(972) 243-5595
www.kimemories.com

Li'l Davis Designs
(480) 223-0080
www.lildavisdesigns.com

LilyPad, The
www.the-lilypad.com

Little Dreamer Designs
www.littledreamerdesigns.com

Luxe Designs
(972) 573-2120
www.luxedesigns.com

Magic Mesh
(651) 345-6374
www.magicmesh.com

Magic Scraps
(904) 482-0092
www.magicscraps.com

Magistical Memories
(818) 842-1540
www.magisticalmemories.com

Making Memories
(801) 294-0430
www.makingmemories.com

Martha Stewart Crafts/Delivery Agent, Inc.
www.marthastewartcrafts.com

May Arts
(800) 442-3950
www.mayarts.com

Maya Road, LLC
(214) 488-3279
www.mayaroad.com

me & my BiG ideas
(949) 583-2065
www.meandmybigideas.com

Michaels Arts & Crafts
(800) 642-4235
www.michaels.com

Microsoft Corporation
www.microsoft.com

Mindy Bush's Photoshop Actions
www.mindysphotoactions.blogspot.com

Mustard Moon
(763) 493-5157
www.mustardmoon.com

My Mind's Eye, Inc.
(800) 665-5116
www.mymindseye.com

Nunn Design
(800) 761-3557
www.nunndesign.com

Offray- see Berwick Offray, LLC

Paper Company, The - see ANW Crestwood

Paper House Productions
(800) 255-7316
www.paperhouseproductions.com

Paper Salon
(800) 627-2648
www.papersalon.com

Paper Studio
(480) 557-5700
www.paperstudio.com

Paper Tapesty
(608) 848-2172
www.papertapestry.com

Polar Bear Press
(801) 451-7670
www.polarbearpress.com

Polka Dot Potato
www.polkadotpotato.com

Pressed Petals
(800) 748-4656
www.pressedpetals.com

Prima Marketing, Inc.
(909) 627-5532
www.primamarketinginc.com

Prism Papers
(866) 902-1002
www.prismpapers.com

Provo Craft
(800) 937-7686
www.provocraft.com

PSX Stamps
www.psxstamps.com

Purple Onion Designs
www.purpleoniondesigns.com

Queen & Co.
(858) 613-7858
www.queenandcompany.com

QuicKutz, Inc.
(888) 702-1146
www.quickutz.com

Reminisce Papers
(319) 358-9777
www.shopreminisce.com

Royal & Langnickel/Royal Brush Mfg.
(800) 247-2211
www.royalbrush.com

Rusty Pickle
(801) 746-1045
www.rustypickle.com

Sakura Hobby Craft
(310) 212-7878
www.sakuracraft.com

Sandylion Sticker Designs
(800) 387-4215
www.sandylion.com

Sassafras Lass
(801) 269-1331
www.sassafraslass.com

Scenic Route Paper Co.
(801) 225-5754
www.scenicroutepaper.com

Scrapbook-Bytes
(607) 642-5391
www.scrapbook-bytes.com

Scrapbook Graphics
www.scrapbookgraphics.com

Scrapworks, LLC / As You Wish Products, LLC
(801) 363-1010
www.scrapworks.com

SEI, Inc.
(800) 333-3279
www.shopsei.com

Sizzix
(877) 355-4766
www.sizzix.com

Stampin' Up!
(800) 782-6787
www.stampinup.com

Staples, Inc.
www.staples.com

Strano Designs
(508) 454-4615
www.stranodesigns.com

Sugar Giggles
www.sugargiggles.com

Sweetwater
(800) 359-3094
www.sweetwaterscrapbook.com

Technique Tuesday, LLC
(503) 644-4073
www.techniquetuesday.com

Tinkering Ink
(877) 727-2784
www.tinkeringink.com

Toastsnatcher
www.toastsnatcher.com

Trim-Tex, Inc.
(800) 874-2333
www.trim-tex.com

Two Peas in a Bucket
(888) 896-7327
www.twopeasinabucket.com

Urban Lily
www.urbanlily.com

We R Memory Keepers, Inc.
(801) 539-5000
www.weronthenet.com

Wrights Ribbon Accents
(877) 597-4448
www.wrights.com

Index

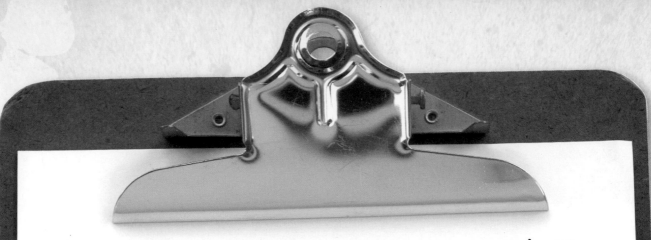

Discover more ways to get inspired and get scrappin' with these amazing titles from Memory Makers Books!

601 Great Scrapbook Ideas

Brimming with inspiration and ideas, you'll discover one amazing page after another in this big book of layouts.

ISBN-13: 978-1-59963-017-5

ISBN-10: 1-59963-017-6

Paperback

272 pages

Z1640

Find Your Groove

Kitty Foster and Wendy McKeehan take you on a journey to discovering your own groovy scrapbook style through quizzes, exercises, challenges and page after page of fabulous layouts sure to inspire.

ISBN-13: 978-1-59963-006-9

ISBN-10: 1-59963-006-0

Paperback

112 pages

Z0787

Paper + Pixels

May Flaum and Audrey Neal teach innovative ways to combine digital scrapbooking with traditional paper crafting.

ISBN-13: 978-1-892127-93-8

ISBN-10: 1-892127-93-8

Paperback with bonus CD-ROM

128 pages

Z0350

These books and other fine Memory Makers titles are available at your local scrapbook or craft retailer or bookstore or from online suppliers.
Visit www.mycraftivity.com and www.memorymakersmagazine.com for more information.